American Rag Dolls

Photographed by
Carol Osbourn

Collection of the late Barbara Graham photographed by husband Robert Graham

American Rag Dolls

Straight From The Heart

Estelle Patino

COLLECTOR BOOKS
A Division of Schroeder Publishing Co., Inc.

The current values in this book should be used only as a guide. They are not intended to set prices, which vary from one section of the country to another. Auction prices as well as dealer prices vary greatly and are affected by condition as well as demand. Neither the Author nor the Publisher assumes responsibility for any losses that might be incurred as a result of consulting this guide.

Additional copies of this book may be ordered from:

Collector Books
P.O. Box 3009
Paducah, KY 42001

@$14.95. Add $1.00 for postage and handling.

Dedication

With All My Love and Gratitude

To my Mom and Dad
Anita and Eugene Caron

For all those long hours spent at
the flea markets!

Acknowledgments

My deepest gratitude and appreciation to all these marvelous people who gave of their precious time and talents:

My photographer, Carol Osbourn, for her patience, perfection and perseverance.

My best friend and mentor, Sandy Thompson, for her optimism and never-ending support.

My friend and client, Mary Worrow, for the use of her wonderful collection.

Robert Graham for all his time and work photographing the collection of his late wife.

Laurie Thompson for the use of her talent.

Marjorie Kimbro for the use of her great collection.

Charlene Lucinian of Pippen Hill Antiques for allowing her dolls to be photographed.

Sue Chalke for her support and encouragement.

Collector Books for giving me the chance to share this with you.

And last, but by no means least, my family; husband Orlando, daughters Kendra, Monica and Carolina (better known as Choc) for allowing me to steal the time to do this!

Contents

Introduction 8
- A Short History of the American Rag Doll 8
- Preservation of the Old Rag Doll 8

Chapter I
- The Primitive 9

Chapter II
- Commercially Made Rag Dolls 30

Chapter III
- Raggedy Ann & Andy 75

Chapter IV
- Rag Dolls Made From 1930s to 1950s 96

Chapter V
- About Reproductions 112

Bibliography 123

Index 124

Price Guide 125

Introduction

Welcome to the realm of the rag doll. In this book I will try to introduce you to her in as much detail as possible. Good old rag dolls are not as readily available as many of the other type of dolls, so the very best must be done with what we have.

The criteria for evaluating a "rag" is not quite the same as with other dolls. Take, for example, the word "mint" (all original, never played with), a word I definitely shy away from when purchasing a rag doll. One must keep in mind that these were the six days a week playthings, not the Sunday afternoon treats. The wear, dust and dirt they possess only add to their charm and is a vital clue to their age. The appeal of the rag does not usually come from its beauty as most appear quite crude, but from the uniqueness, construction, amount of character, detailing or sometimes lack of it and quality of workmanship. It is almost like looking over an old quilt.

The best and safest way to acquire a nice old rag doll is, of course, from the family of the original owner. But as is known, this is also the most difficult. So the next best is the estate sale, garage sale or local flea market. Dealers who have been selling rags over a number of years are usually quite knowledgeable, but those who have just started have a lot to learn. So Buyer, do please beware. I hope that this book will at least make that "beware" a little less intimidating.

The value of the dolls is given as the actual worth on the open market. As we all have learned at one time or another, the so-called "book price" is not always the selling price. The values are based on auction prices, doll shows, prices of folk art and American textiles. Unfortunately for the collector, there has been a tremendous upsurge in prices due to the large interest in country primitives.

It is wise to remember that these dolls are an actual part of our history and may not be as good a monetary investment as a historical one, one that comes straight from the heart.

A Short History of the American Rag Doll

The rag doll is known universally, but for America it has become a part of history. It has been raised to the level of folk art, making it a true part of our heritage.

Long before the settlers came, the Indians were busy sewing rag dolls. As the 13 colonies were founded, the rag doll was in the making. It crossed prairies, mountains and deserts. It survived three wars, and was always there to comfort loving little owners when nothing else could easily be obtained. Because of all these hardships that had to be endured, the rag doll that was made before 1850 and has survived is a rare breed. Luckily, however, some did make it through, enough to tell us much about the attitudes of those times. The rag doll appears to have flourished during this country's periods of strife, for she was always there, readily made from the simplest of materials. She was even instrumental in giving jobs to the needy during the Depression era (the WPA) and in aiding to raise funds for many of the churches (Beecher, Presbyterian, Moravian). It's no wonder that as early as 1870 she was elevated to the status of becoming patented. From then on it was uphill.

It is now certain that the first dolls played with by colonial children were not imported from Europe, but were most definitely homemade.

Preservation of the Old Rag Doll

Preserving an old rag doll is really not that complicated. Since an average house is not equipped with special lighting or humidity control, the best place to keep the dolls is in a cabinet. However, many times collectors enjoy having the dolls sitting out around the house. I have never found this to be detrimental if the dolls are kept clean, out of direct light and away from vents. A few odorless moth balls under the clothes or in the cabinets is never a bad idea. Moths like to eat dirt, not fabric, so it is adviseable to launder (by hand) the clothing using a mild detergent. This should not be done if there is any fraying or deterioration of the fabric. Fraying can be arrested by backing the affected spot with an old piece of matching fabric using a fabric glue. Always try to keep as much of the original as possible. If a doll absolutely needs re-dressing, then a dress from the same period as the doll is vital to preserve her charm, as well as her value. It is important to keep in mind that the more original the doll, the greater the value.

Cleaning the doll itself, if it is a very old one, should best be left alone. Dolls such as the Alabama and the Chase can be wiped off using a product such as Kleen & Shine. Never use soap and water. Never try this if the doll shows signs of flaking or peeling and above all, never re-paint. A re-painted doll has lost its originality, not to mention its value. Repairing torn-off limbs or tears on the body with old cotton thread or fabric glue is a good idea.

The key idea in preservation is restoration, to return the doll to as near its original state as possible without the addition of any new substances. Oh, just one more thing, investing in a good feather duster is highly recommended!

Chapter I

The Primitive

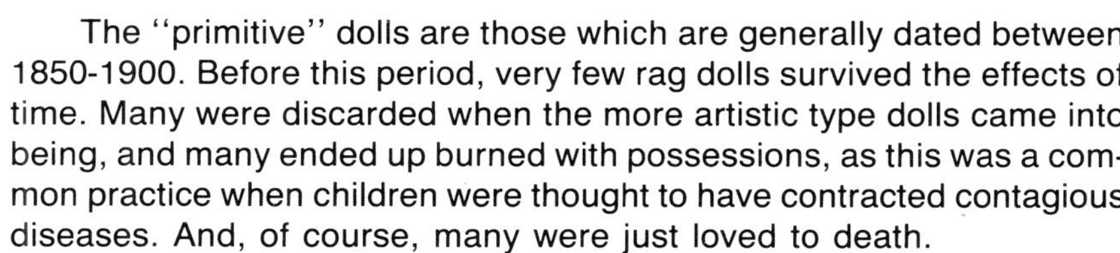

The "primitive" dolls are those which are generally dated between 1850-1900. Before this period, very few rag dolls survived the effects of time. Many were discarded when the more artistic type dolls came into being, and many ended up burned with possessions, as this was a common practice when children were thought to have contracted contagious diseases. And, of course, many were just loved to death.

To try and accurately date the treasures that have survived is nearly impossible, as not much importance was placed on these everyday playthings, and many were one of a kind. But there are some clues that do help to approximate an age. Construction is one. The construction of a rag varied with the mother's imagination and the type of textiles available at the time. Fabrics most often used during this period were unbleached cotton, muslin, twill, wool, stockingnette, oilcloth and burlap. Stuffing most often consisted of heavy cotton batting, sawdust, bran, milkweed, scraps of materials, straw and sometimes dried beans were mixed in. Facial features of a doll were either stitched or painted with substances such as beet juice, squid ink (sepia), charred coal, house paints and oil paints. The hair was either painted on or wigs were stitched on. Animal, as well as human hair, was used to make the wigs, which were usually sparse. The hair was sometimes applied directly to the head by a technique known as "plating" (working into small braids then sewn onto the head.)

The heads and bodies are found in all different shapes, most being out of proportion. Early heads were flat with flat faces, egg shaped, flat front, rounded back, elongated, flat topped and triangular.

Bodies can either be plump or shapely. Hands may have stitched fingers, mitts or stumps. Feet, if they exist, are usually crudely done, assuming a first ballet position or just simply sticking straight out. A few examples have old velvet boots with cross stitching sewn on.

The clothes they wear directly reflects the times and the status of the family they came from. Anything from simple work clothes to elaborate ladies trousseau can be found. But no matter what their beginnings or physical faults, they were always loved. A good point to keep in mind when looking for one!

Author's Collection

Type: Lifesize Rag Baby, circa Civil War period

Construction: *Body* - layers of muslin wrapped upon itself (no stuffing), stitched belly button; *Hands* - stockingnette over muslin, separate fingers; *Feet* - stockingnette over muslin, stitched toes; *Features* - molded, including the tongue, appears to be colored with a type of dye; the ears are applied; *Hair* - human, applied by plating; *Head* - applied separately, doll is quite heavy; *Clothes* - original to doll

Clues to Dating: Wrap type construction, negroid features on a definitely caucasian doll (? made by black mammy)

Author's Collection

Type: 30'' Turn of Century Oil Painted Rag

Construction: *Body* - cotton stuffed with cotton, jointed at knees, hips and shoulders; *Hands* - mitts with free standing thumbs; *Feet* - large stubs; *Features* - oil painted on a flat face, head is rounded only in the back; a seam runs from one side of the head to the other and down the middle of the back; no ears; *Clothes* - not original but old and of the period

Clues to Dating: type of head construction, materials used

Author's Collection

Type: 36" Turn of Century Oil Painted Rag

Construction: *Body* - cotton fabric stuffed with straw; jointed at hips and shoulders; *Hands* - separate fingers; *Feet* - stubs; *Features* - oil painted on a flat face; head is rounded in the back only; no ears; *Clothes* - dress may be original

Clues to Dating: construction of the head, materials used; doll very impressive in this large size

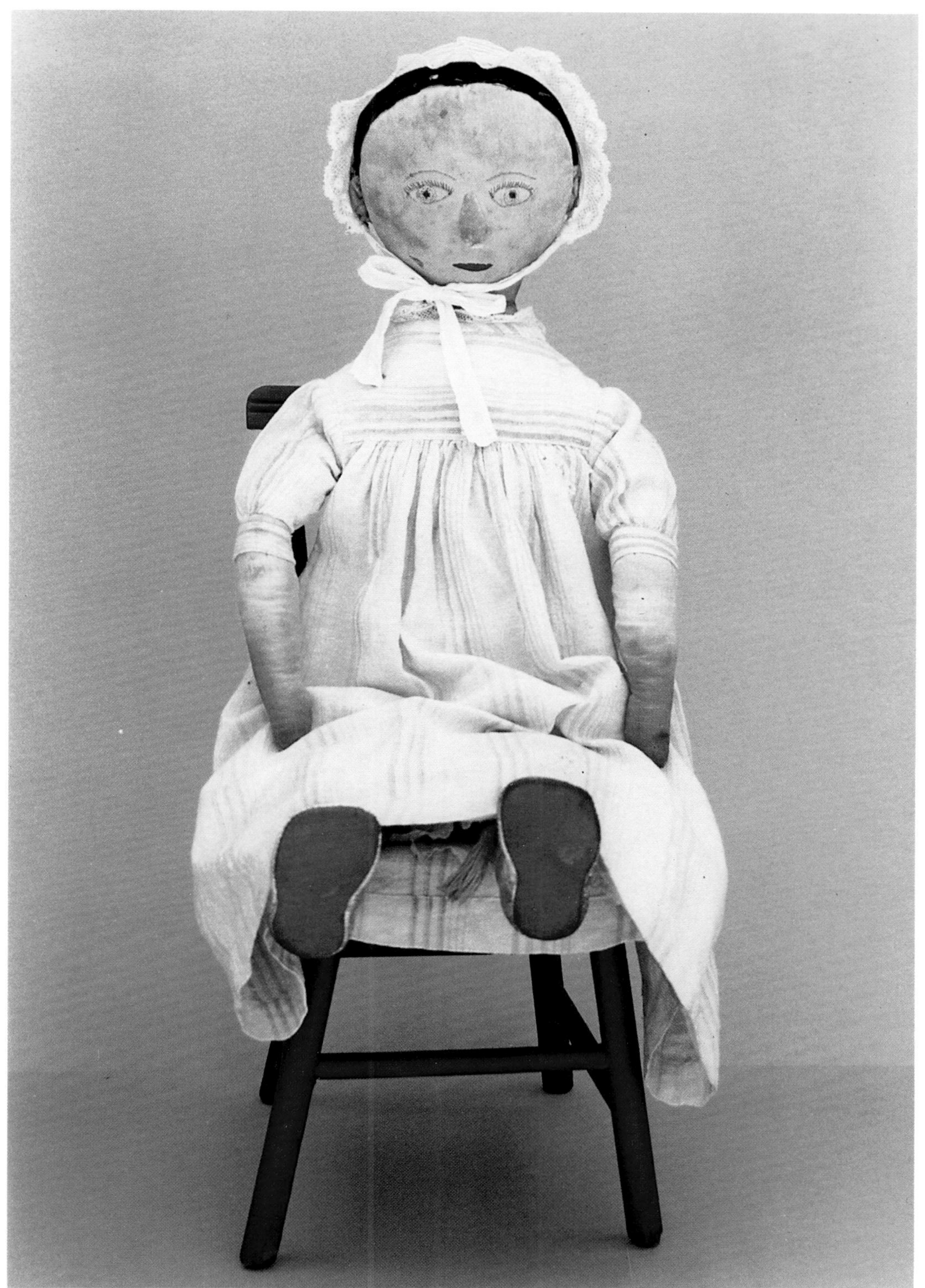

Author's Collection

Type: 24" Turn of the Century Rag Doll
Construction: *Body* - unbleached cotton stuffed with cotton; jointed at shoulders, knees and hips; hands are stubs; *Features* - stitched, nose is applied as well as the ears; *Hair* - old stocking material sewn onto the head; *Clothes* - old

Author's Collection

Type: 17" Late 1800s Oil Painted Rag Doll
Construction: *Body* - polished type cotton stuffed with cotton; jointed at shoulders only; hands are stubs, feet pointed outward; *Features* - finely oil painted; *Hair* - partially oil painted; has a piece of human hair sewn across top of head; *Clothes* - original

Author's Collection

Type: 18" Late 1800s Rag Doll
Construction: *Body* - cotton stuffed with cotton; not jointed; *Hands* - well-formed with separately stitched fingers; *Feet* - stubs; *Features* - barely visible done in pencil; head is made with four seams; completely rounded, no hair; *Clothes* - may be original
Clues to Dating: overall construction

Author's Collection

Type: 17" Mid 1800s Rag
Construction: *Body* - unbleached muslin stuffed with cotton and pieces of cloth; jointed at hips and shoulders; *Hands* - stubs; *Feet* - stubs; *Features* - done in vegetable dye; head is flat back and front; no hair; *Clothes* - dress and underclothes are original
Clues to Dating: materials used (for facial features)

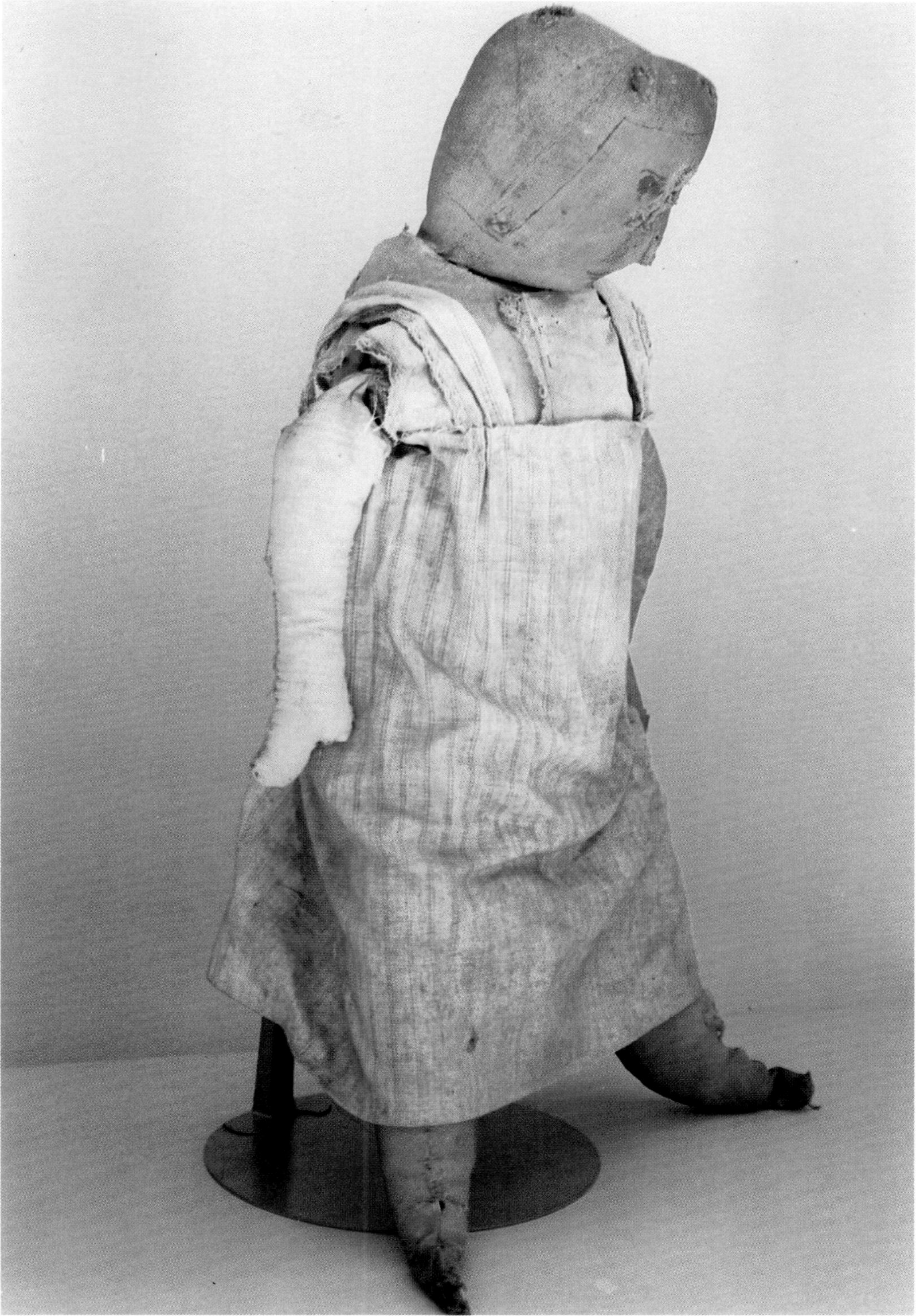

Collection of Charlene Lucinian

Type: 22'' Primitive Rag Doll
Construction: *Body* - unbleached cotton stuffed with old cotton; jointed at shoulders; hands are stubs; feet point outward; *Features* - drawn with ink; nose and chin are molded; head is made in three parts; no hair; *Clothes* - original

Collection of Charlene Lucinian

Type: 14" Early Black Rag Doll Circa 1900s
Construction: *Body* - Muslin stuffed with cotton; not jointed; *Features* - stitched, has stitched fingers; *Hair* - sparse wool yarn; *Clothes* - original

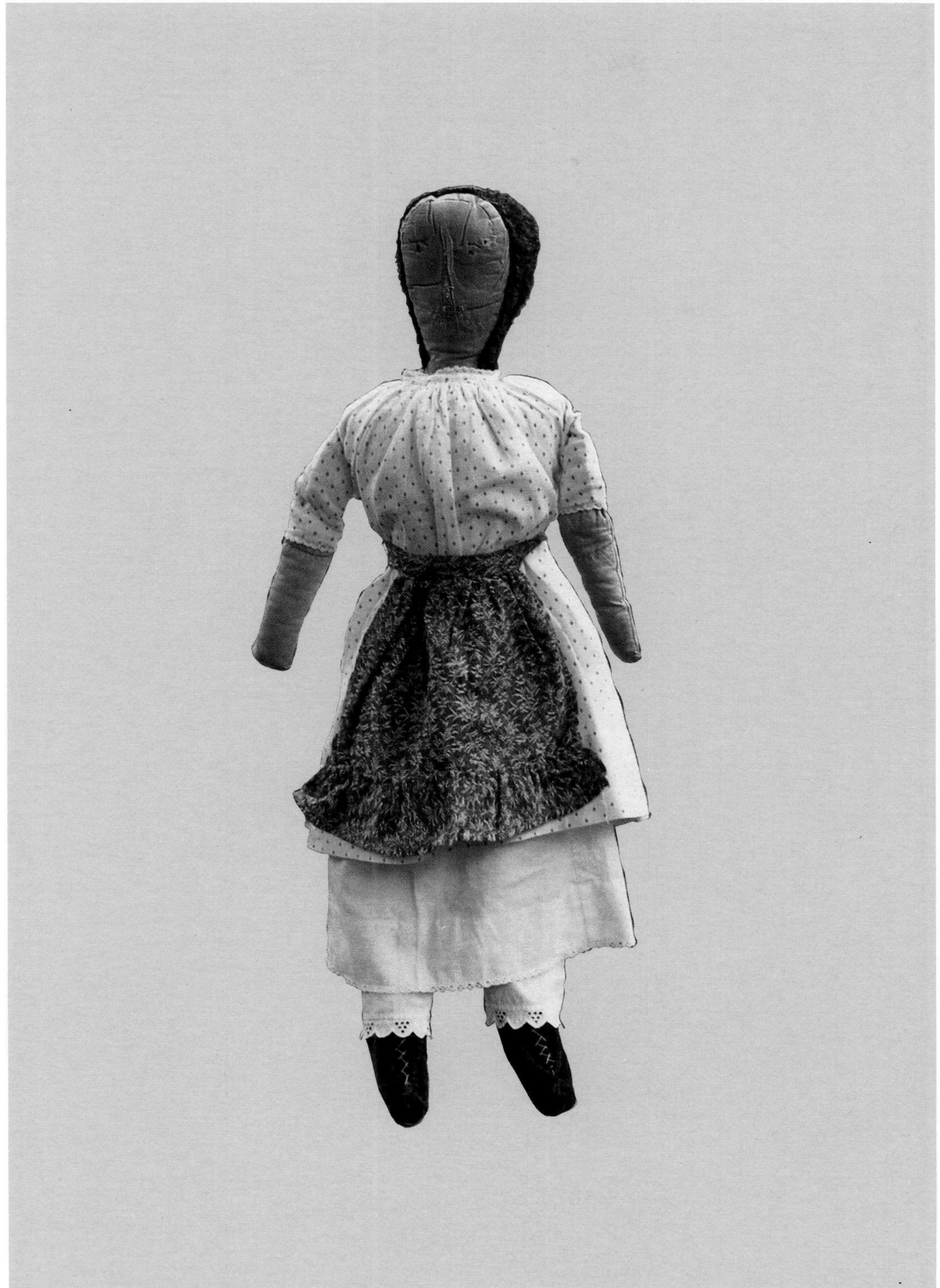

Collection of Elizabeth Folse

Type: 22" Primitive Homemade Rag Doll
Construction: *Body* - unbleached cotton stuffed with old cotton batting; stubs for hands; sewed on velvet boots with lacing; *Features* - stitched; *Hair* - old mohair type fabric stitched directly to the head

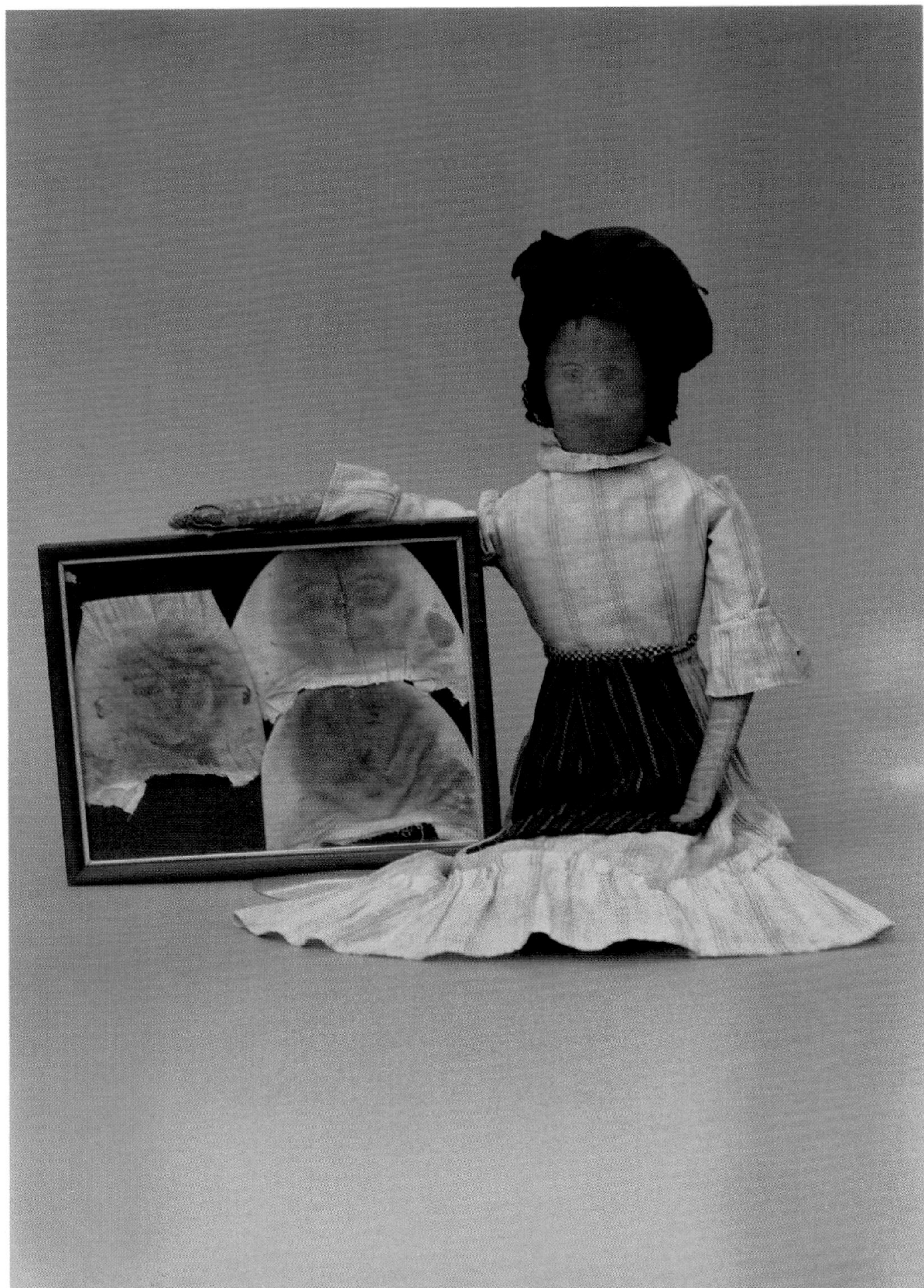

Author's Collection

Type: 23'' 1870s Multi-Faced Rag
Construction: *Body* - cotton stuffed with cotton; jointed at knees, hips and shoulders; *Hands* - mitts with stitched thumbs; *Feet* - stubs; *Features* - pencil drawn, head is egg-shaped with dowel down through neck into body; *Extra Faces* - cotton with pencil-drawn features; *Clothes* - dress and apron original to the doll; bonnet added
Clues to Dating: construction of head using dowel

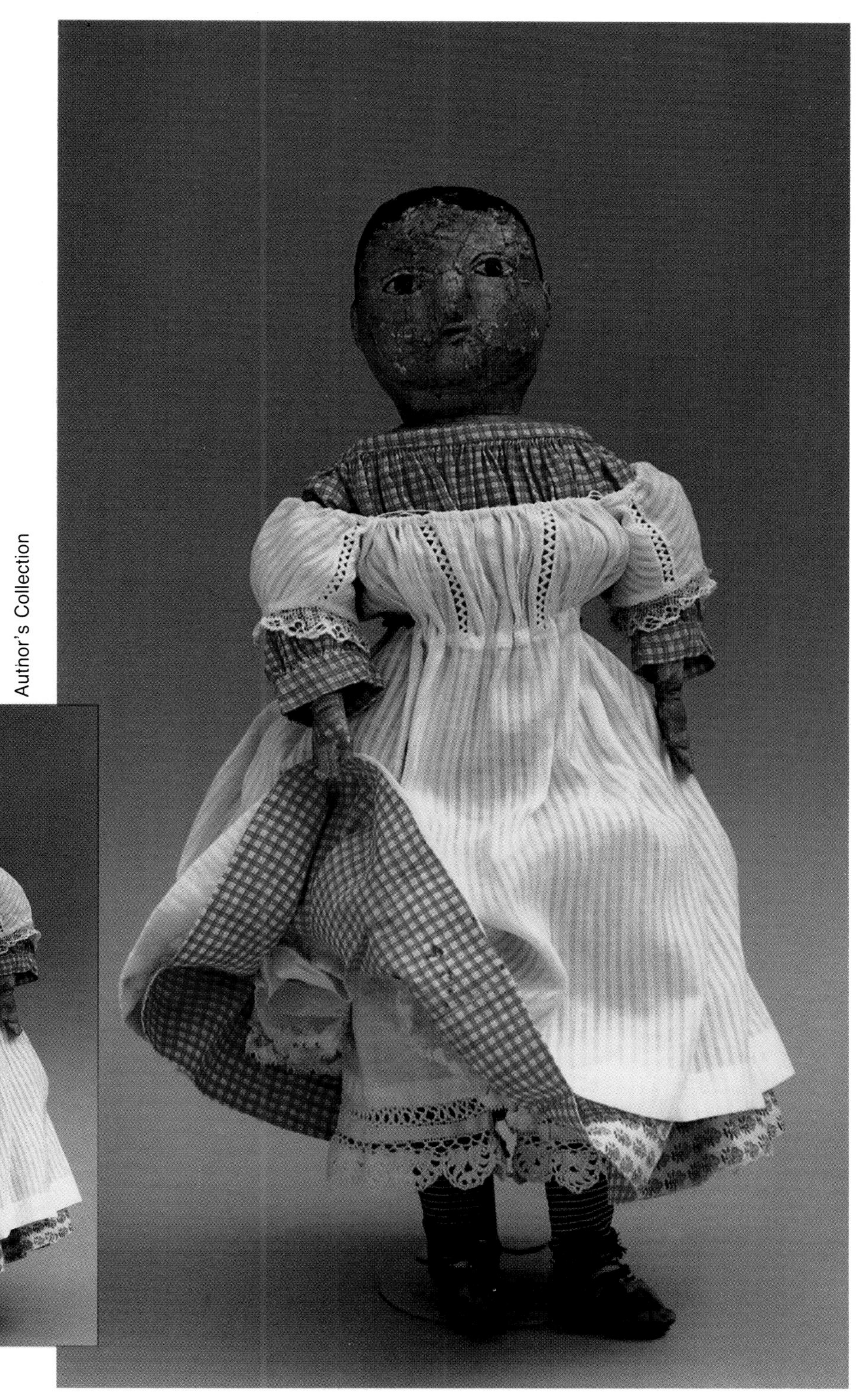

Author's Collection

Type: 20" 1870s Oil Painted Rag ? Izannah Walker

Construction: *Body* - cotton stuffed with cotton; jointed at knees, hips and shoulders; *Hands* - stitched fingers, free standing thumb (oil painted to mid arm); *Feet* - stubs; *Features* - molded and oil painted; ears are applied; head is fully rounded; *Clothes* - old, not original

Clues to Dating: very specific type of construction. This doll has had much repair over the years and has lost some of the more familiar Izannah Walker traits. However, construction is of the basic Walker type.

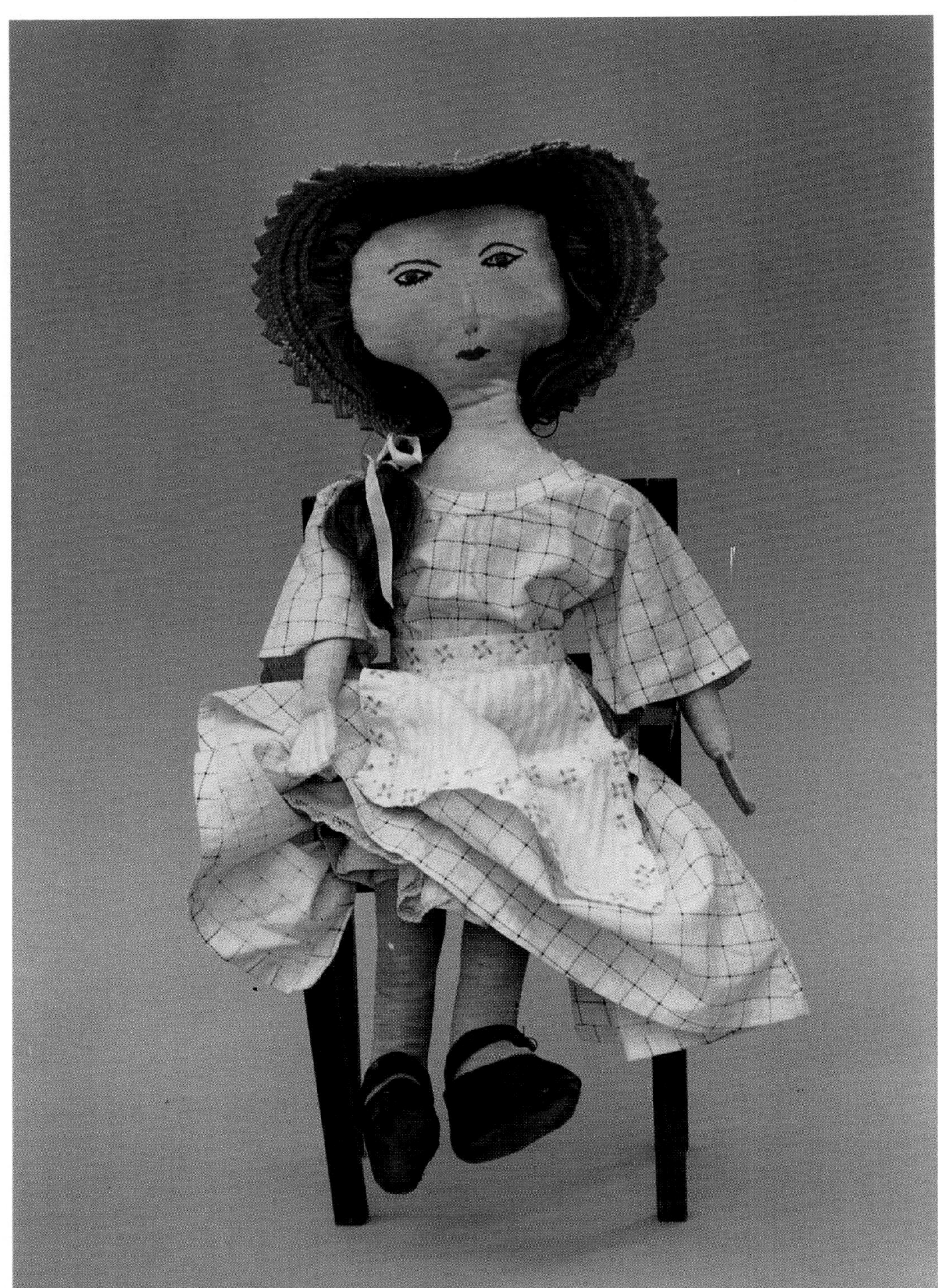

Author's Collection

Type: 21'' Early 1900s Rag

Construction: *Body* - unbleached cotton stuffed with cotton; jointed at hips, knees and shoulders; *Hands* - crudely stitched fingers; *Feet* - stubs; *Features* - nose is molded by stitching; wig is made of human hair; head is square in appearance and flat; *Clothes* - dress may be original

Clues to Dating: type of head construction

Author's Collection

Type: 18'' Early 1900s Oil Painted Rag
Construction: *Body* - cotton stuffed with cotton; jointed at hips and shoulders; *Hands* - stitched fingers with free standing thumbs; *Feet* - velvet shoes stitched on; *Features* - painted in oils directly onto the fabric; nose and chin are molded with a seam running down the center of the face; head is rounded; no hair; *Clothes* - not original
Clues to Dating: materials used, overall construction

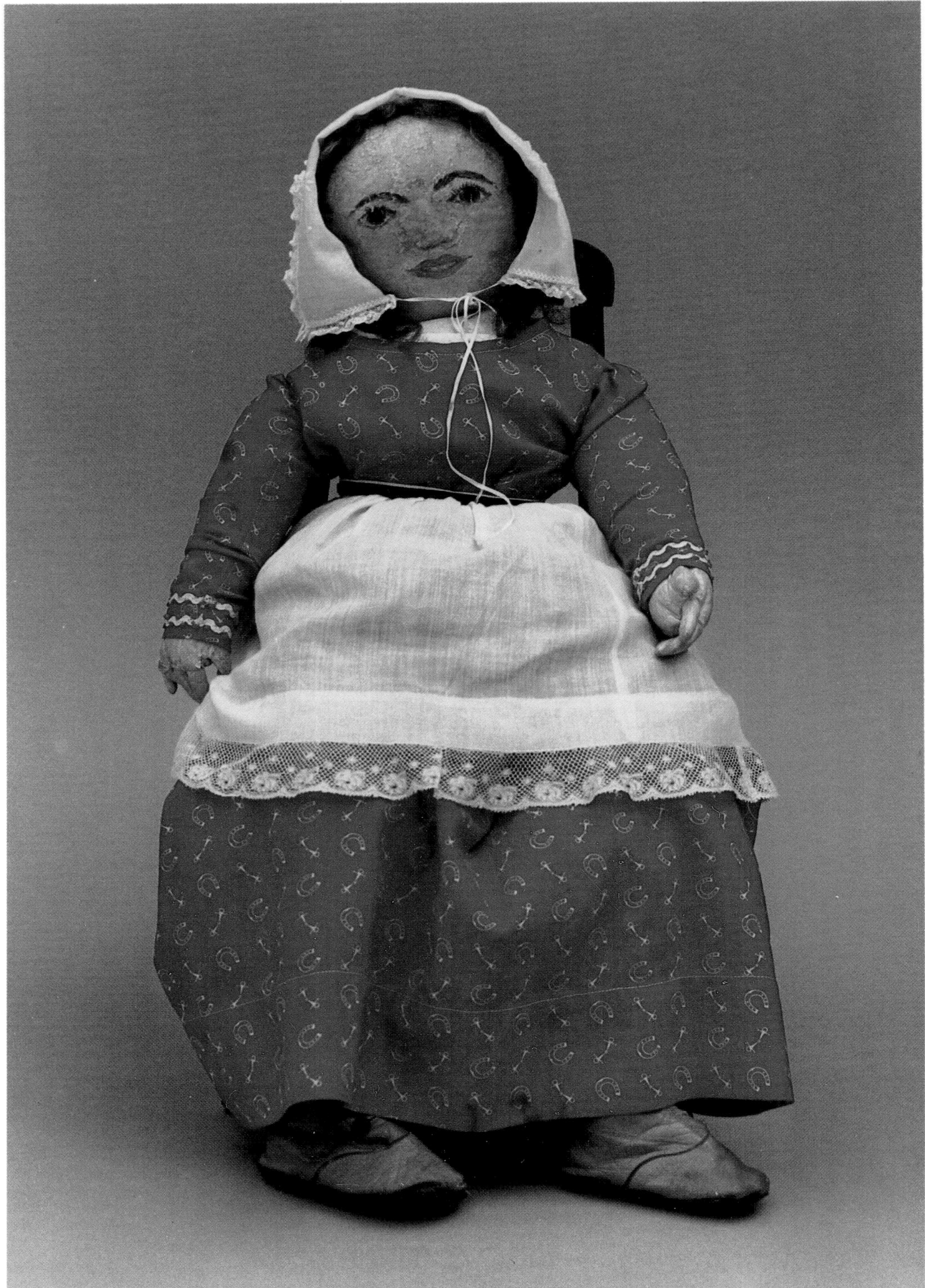

Collection of Mary Worrow

Type: 30" Mid 1900s Painted Rag Lady
Construction: *Body* - heavy cotton stuffed with cotton; jointed at shoulders, hips and knees; *Hands* - painted and have individually stitched fingers; *Feet* - stubs; *Features* - nose appears to be molded with gesso type material; face is crudely painted with house-type paint; *Clothes* - old, not original

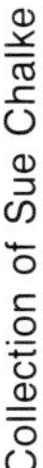
Collection of Sue Chalke

Type: 25'' Late 1800s Oil Painted Rag
Construction: *Body* - unbleached cotton stuffed with cotton; jointed at the shoulders and hips; *Hands* - painted mitts; *Features* - very artistically oil painted; note the smiling mouth with teeth; *Clothes* - old

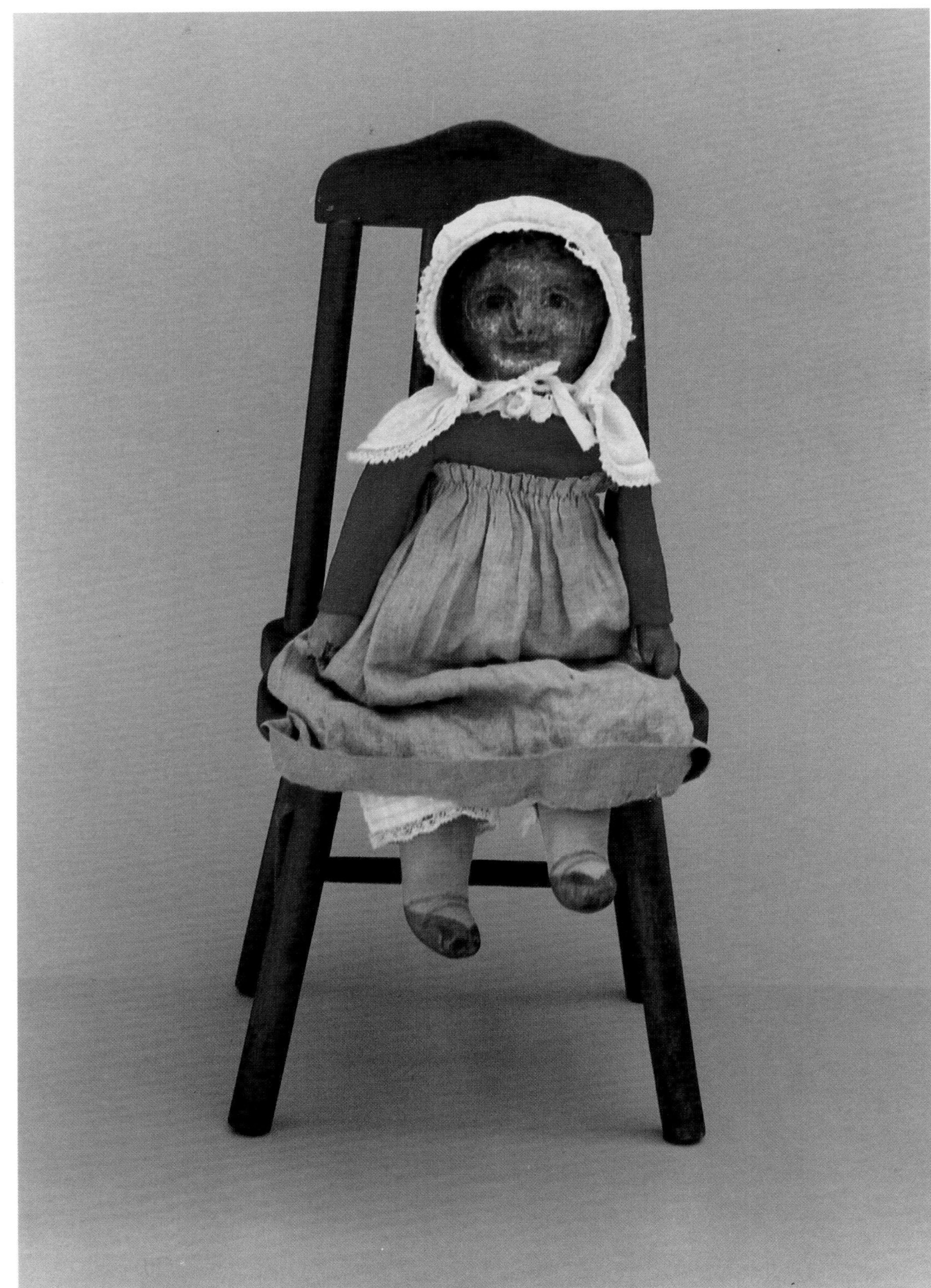
Collection of Mary Worrow

Type: 17'' Turn of Century Oil Painted Rag
Construction: *Body* - muslin stuffed with bran; jointed at shoulders, hips and knees; *Hands* - painted mitts; *Feet* - painted on shoes; *Features* - flat oil painted; *Clothes* - dress is original to the doll

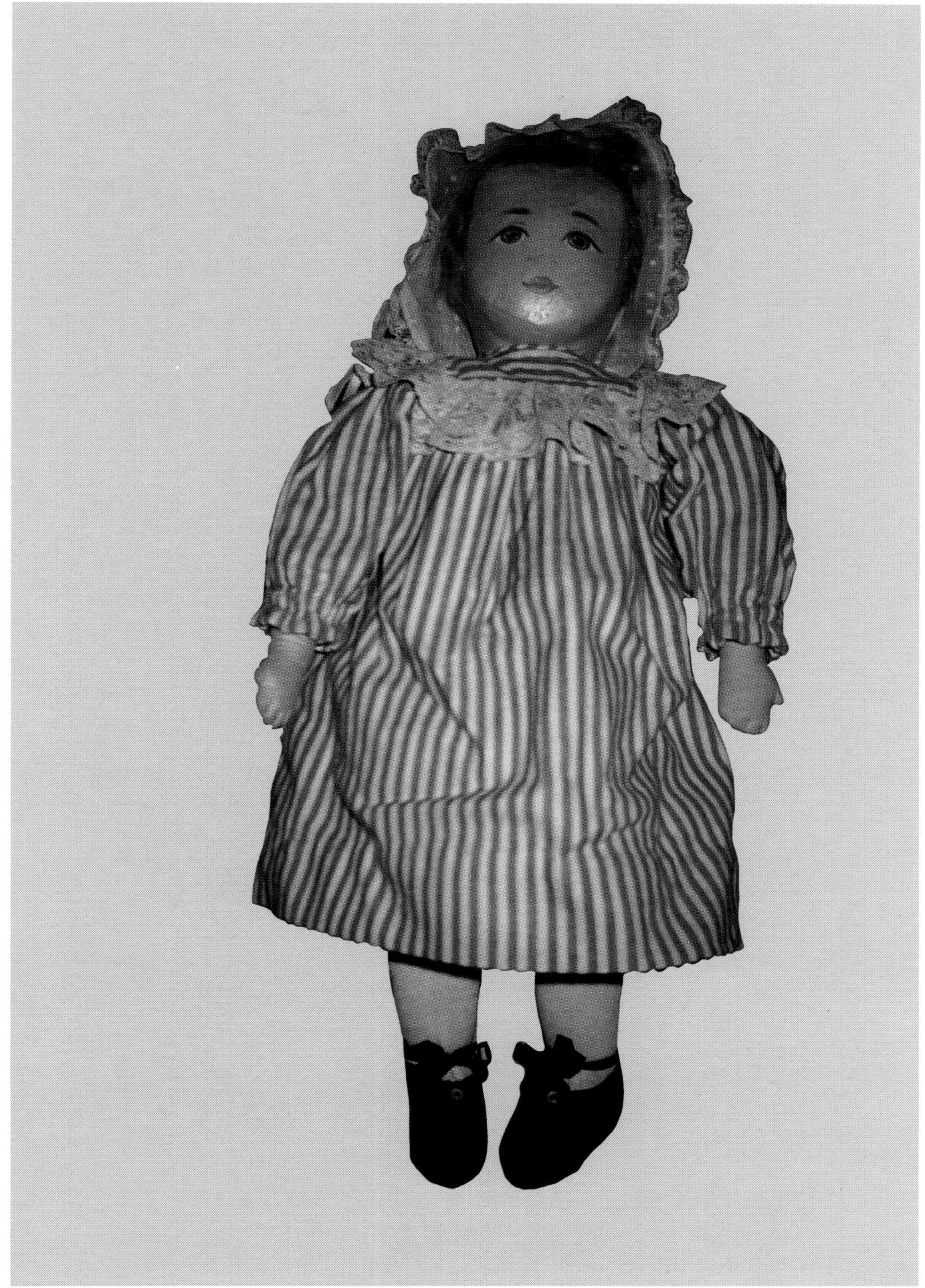

Collection of the late Barbara Graham

Type: 22" Oil painted rag circa Early 1900s
Construction: *Body* - cotton jointed at shoulders and hips; *Hands* - stitched fingers crudely done; *Features* - painted, with molded chin; sparse human hair applied; *Clothes* - old

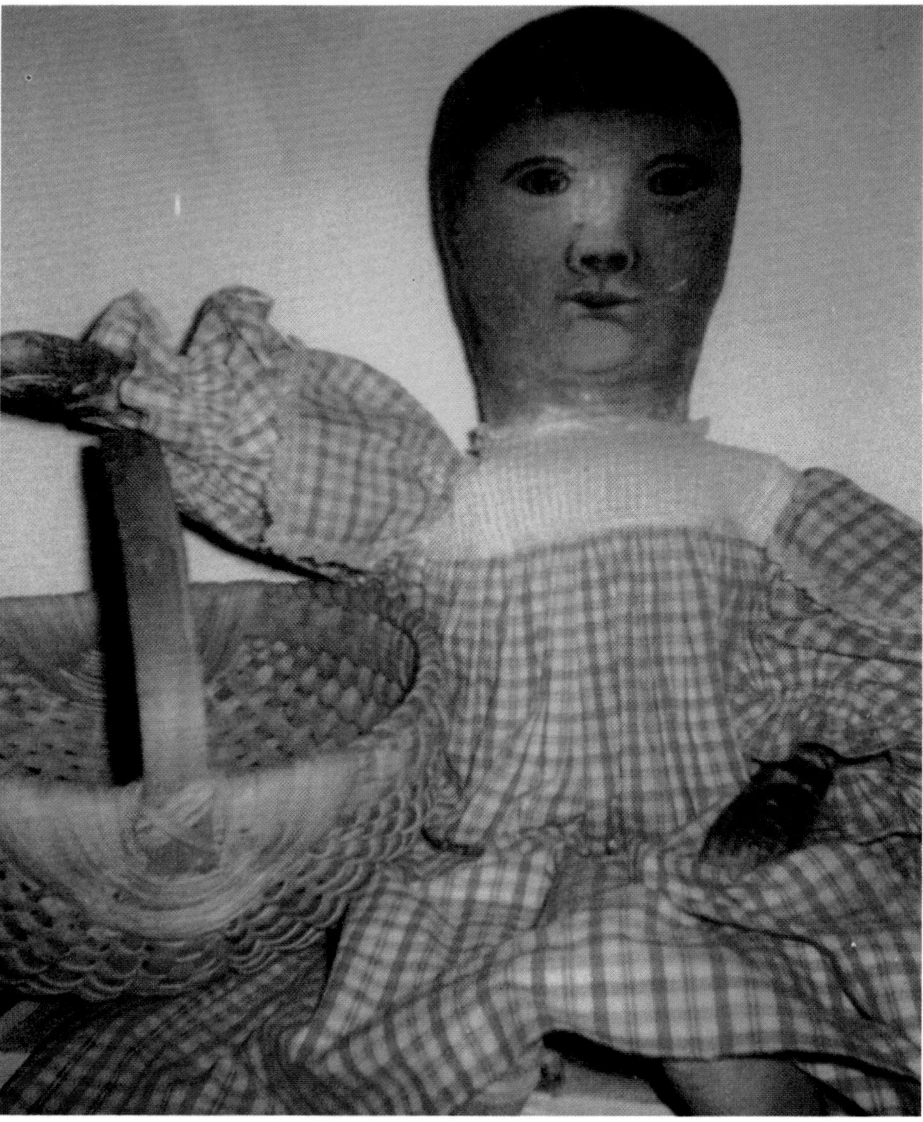

Collection of Sue Chalke

Type: 23" Mid 1800s Oil Painted Rag Doll
Construction: *Body* - cotton stuffed with cotton; not in proportion with the head; jointed at hips and shoulders; *Hands* - mitts; *Feet* - stubs; *Features* - exaggerated; oil painted; head is large egg shape; *Clothes* - not original
Clues to Dating: overall construction, very early type

These very early genuine primitives can almost command their own price.

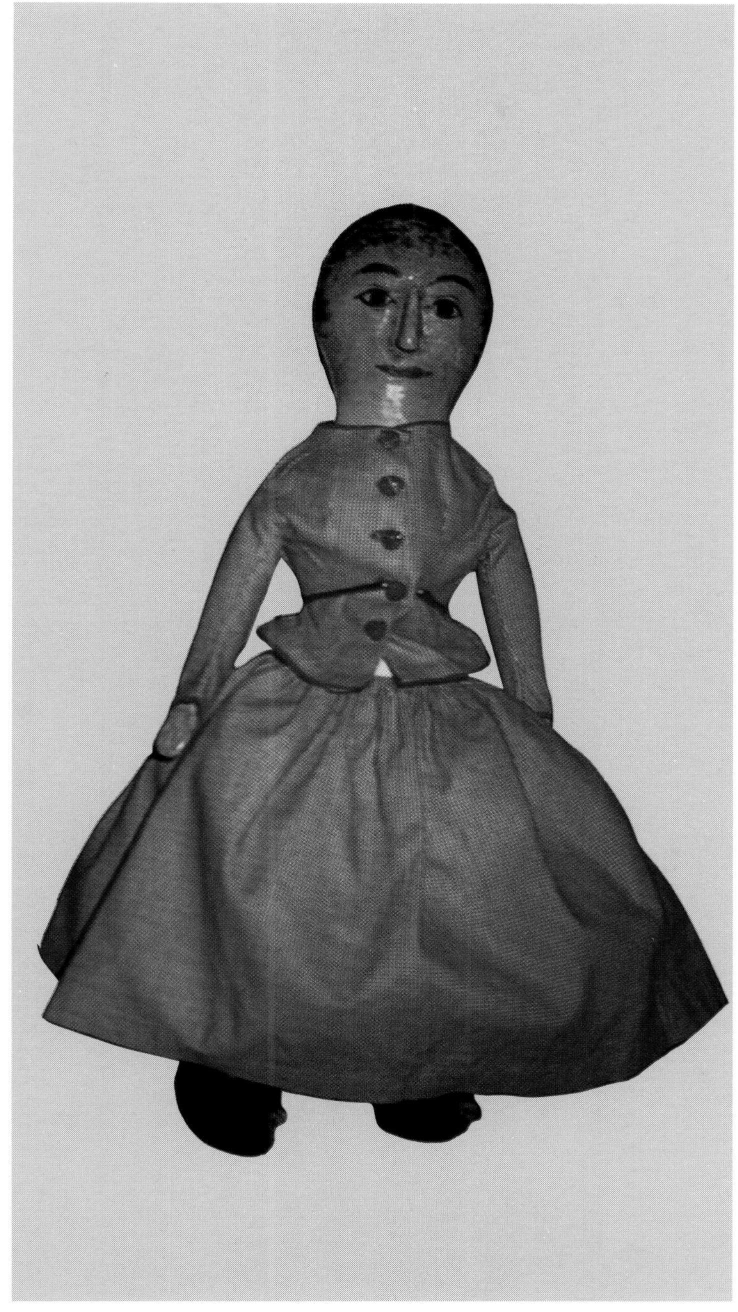

Collection of the late Barbara Graham

Type: 17" Oil Painted Rag Doll Circa Mid 1800s
Construction: *Body* - muslin; *Hands* - mitts; *Features* - oil painted with applied nose; *Limbs* - painted with painted shoes and stockings; *Clothes* - old
Clues to Dating: simple old-style construction

Chapter II

Commercially Made Rag Dolls

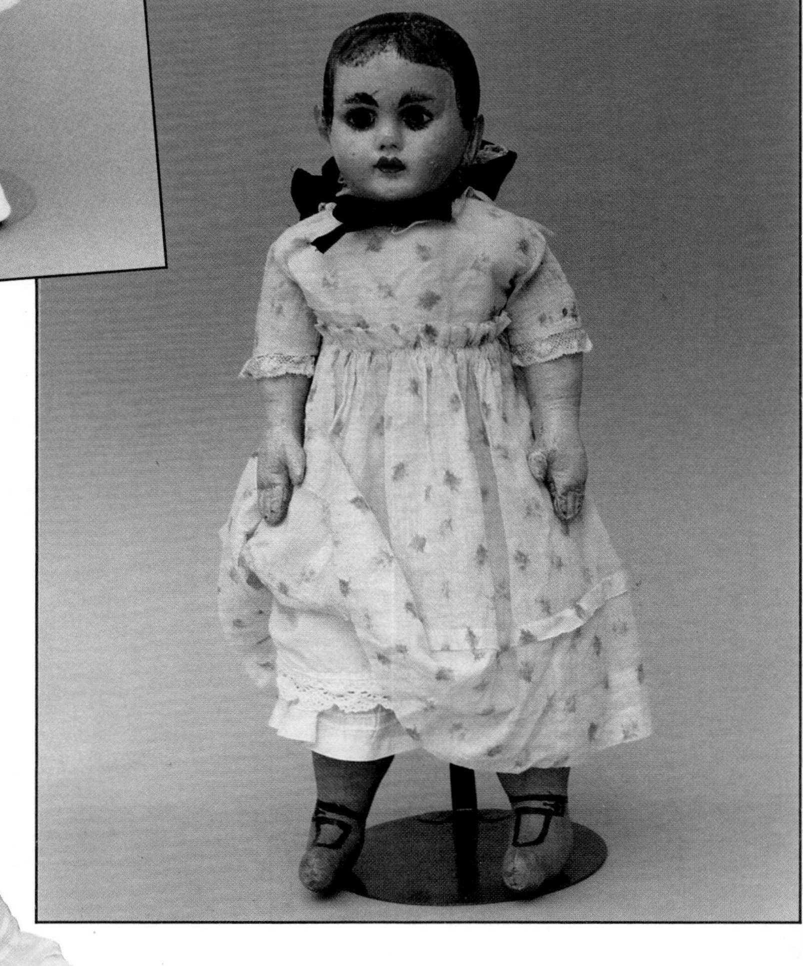

This chapter deals with the doll upon which the maker has left his mark. Most of these dolls are so distinctive that even when the mark is no longer visible, they are still very identifyable.

Commercial Manufacturers of Rag Dolls

The Alabama Baby

Alabama Babies were made in Roanoke, Alabama by Ella Gant Smith from 1900 to 1925. Approximately 8,000 dolls were produced each year. They ranged from 12" to 17" and there were 11 patents taken on this doll.

The earlier dolls are always differentiated by the way in which the crown was stitched to the top of the head and the applied ears. In the later mold, the head was all one piece.

The different types of Alabama Babies include a black version, barefoot version and wigged version. The faces are all different because each was hand-painted by different individuals. The painted shoes also vary in style. Some are blue or brown Mary Janes. Others are blue or brown high tops. They can either be painted to almost the top of the leg or just above the ankle. The body type seems to remain the same on all the dolls. The hands are large with fingers that are stitched but not separate except for the thumb. Separate fingers have been found on some of the large early versions.

A question often asked when collecting this type of doll is "is the mark necessary to the value of the doll?" The answer is no, because the unique construction of this doll is its own mark.

Art Fabric Mills

Art Fabric Mills of New York printed sheets of rag dolls from 1900 until 1910. These are known as lithographs. Many types of these were printed. They included girl dolls, boy dolls, baby dolls, black dolls and some animals.

The mark on these can usually be found beneath the foot and along the seams. However, many times it was sewn into the seam or completely cut off.

A life size "French doll" was put out in 1901. She was done on heavy sateen with red stockings and black shoes.

Many Art Fabrics are still available but the condition varies greatly according to the fabric on which they were printed, some being a lot heavier than others.

Miscellaneous Lithographs

Also included in this section will be other examples of lithographed dolls. There were many American companies that were producing this type doll during this period. It is very difficult to try and identify all of these as the mark was usually cut away when the dolls were assembled.

Babyland Rag

Babyland rags were produced by Horsman Co. from 1893 until 1928. The early dolls had painted faces, the later ones were lithographed. They ranged in size from 12" to 30". No mark is found on the dolls.

The types made were quite varied. They included babies, boys, girls, black dolls, characters (Buster Brown, Red Riding Hood). They are rather attractive dolls and the original clothes are desirable on these dolls. Also, the larger ones are harder to find.

The faces of these dolls are not painted or printed directly onto the head. They are done on a separate piece of material which is then applied over the head. The hair on the bonnet dolls is not a full wig, but rather a piece sewn just around the face. Another point of interest is that on the smaller dolls, the hands are mitts with free standing thumbs and on the larger dolls, the fingers are stitched and the arms are jointed at the elbows.

Missionary Rag Baby

The Missionary Rag Baby was created by Julia Beecher in 1885. It was sold to help raise monies for the church's missions. Production lasted until 1905.

This doll came in sizes from 16" to 23" and is affectionately known as the first Cabbage Patch Kid. It was made of either pink or black stockingnette. The depth of the face was created with expert needlework sculpturing forming ears, nose and eyes. The features were then oil painted. Brown eyes tend to be rarer. There was a variation in the construction of the hands; some had outstretched fingers, while on others they were clenched. The toes were stitched and the knees jointed. The hair was made of soft yellow wool loops that had a tendency to change to a soft beige with the effects of time. The doll was generally clothed in a baby dress and bonnet of the period.

There is another type doll attributed to Mrs. Beecher. It is a black doll and is constructed entirely differently from

the latter. The only part of the doll that is stockingnette is the head. The rest of the body is a dull chocolate brown sateen with mitt hands and is jointed at the knees. A wig of closely knotted black wool yarn is attached to the head. The nose and cheeks are molded. Thick red lips are embroidered and the eyes are made from shoe button type beads mounted on a shell-like substance which forms the whites of the eyes.

This is a very well made doll. Beecher dolls are rare as not too many of them survived the loving.

Bruckner

This doll was manufactured by Albert Bruckner from 1901 until 1930. It came in sizes from 12" to 31". The most common sizes found are the 12 and 14 inch.

The Bruckner is very often confused with the Babyland. The face of the Bruckner is a lithographed mask applied to the head by stitching. The mark is usually found in the lower corner of this mask. This doll is not as well made as the Babyland, nor as desirable.

Chase Doll

The Chase is another cottage industry doll. Martha Jenks Chase, from Pawtucket, R.I. began making her dolls in 1889. They continued to be made until 1930.

The early dolls are made of molded stockingnette with sateen bodies which are jointed at the elbows and knees. The mark is found stamped on the lower hip. They range in size from 8" to 30", the smallest being the hardest to find.

A question often asked concerning the Chase is "which came first, the mannikins or the dolls?" The dolls were manufactured first, then came the mannikins which were used for hospital training purposes. It is fairly simple to differentiate the two. The mannikins are lifesize, extremely heavy and fully painted, including the bodies and are often found having pierced nostrils.

In 1905, Mrs. Chase put out a line of character dolls. These included Alice in Wonderland, Mad Hatter, Tweedle Dee and Dum, the Duchess and the rabbit. Some others included a Mammy nurse, two pickaninies and some Charles Dickens characters. In 1908, George Washington was created. He was 25" tall.

The clothes on the Chase dolls were fashioned from children's clothes of the period. Boy dolls wore rompers and girl dolls wore dresses made with tucking and smocking.

Many beginner collectors, upon finding a Chase doll, think immediately that it has been repainted. This is due to the technique employed by Mrs. Chase called "impasto" painting (leaving ridges of paint, especially on the hair). They also tend to retain their vibrant colors as waterproof sealer was used to protect them.

The Chase dolls not only made an important contribution to the world of play, but also became a vital teaching aid in the world of medicine. They are a definite asset to any collection.

Columbian Doll

The Columbian Doll holds a high place in any collection. She possesses a unique charm, as well as artistic charisma. The Columbian was created by Emma E. Adams of Oswego, New York in 1892. They range in size from 15" to 29". Boy, girl, and baby dolls were made, including several black dolls. All were individually hand-painted by either Emma or local artists employed by her. Emma's sister, Marietta, was responsible for dressing the dolls. The clothing seems to have set the price of the doll rather than the size. Girls were dressed in either pink or blue gingham dresses, bonnets and hand-sewn kid slippers. Babies were in dresses of white, pink or blue with bonnets and crocheted booties. Boys had shirts with feather stitching, royal blue or navy trousers equipped with twill cross over straps to hold them up. All were skillfully made.

In 1893, the doll received the name Columbian when it gained admittance to the Columbian Exposition of the Chicago World's Fair. In 1894, a diploma of honorable mention was awarded to Emma by the Columbian Commission.

The Columbian was never patented. It was simply marked with a rubber stamp on the lower torso. It read "Columbian Doll/Emma E. Adams; Oswego Center/N.Y.

After 1906 and the death of Emma, the mark was changed to, "The Columbian Doll Manufactured by Marietta Adams Ruttan Oswego, N.Y."

It is certain, however, that many dolls were made before the stamp came into use. It is not unlikely, therefore, to find an early doll with no mark.

Maude Tausy Fangle

Maude Tausy Fangle designed dolls from 1920 until 1930. They had flat lithographed faces. One was a 14" baby, the other one was manufactured by Georgene Novelty Co. and named Sweets. These dolls came either dressed with removable clothing or printed bodies. The ones having the clothing are more desirable. A difficult doll to find.

Ida Gutsell

This doll was patented by Ida Gutsell of Ithica, N.Y. in 1883 and manufactured by Cocheco Manufacturing Co. Unlike other lithograph dolls of the period, this one was three dimensional, having a seam down the center of the face and a pattern included for outer clothes. It is 16" tall. Not an attractive doll, but an interesting one.

Kamkins

Kamkins is one of the commercially made rag dolls. They were made by Louise R. Kampes from 1919 to 1928 in Atlantic City, New Jersey. There appears to have been two sizes produced, an 18" and a 19". The 18" was marked with a heart on the chest. The 19" was marked on the back of the head and had a voice box. This doll also came with different style wigs if requested by the customer, but the most often found is the short pixie style.

The wardrobe for the Kamkins was extensive. Outfits for every season of the year as well as playclothes were available.

The workmanship found on these dolls is excellent.

Mother Congress Doll

The Mother Congress Doll was patented by Madge L. Mead of Philadelphia, Penn. on Nov. 6, 1900. It was manufactured by the Mother Congress Doll Co. of Philadelphia.

This is a rather difficult doll to find as they were not very durable. The facial features are lithographed on a round head, instead of flat. The hair is blonde with a blue bow and the doll wears black Mary Jane-style shoes. She comes fully marked on the front torso and is also known as Baby Stuart.

Moravian

The Moravian doll, also known as the Polly Heckewelder, was created and used to raise funds for the church. She was made by the older sisters of the Ladies Sewing Society of the Central Moravian Church, Bethlehem, Pennsylvania in 1872. The doll was named Polly Heckewelder after the daughter of a missionary. She was said to have been the first white girl born in the Ohio region at that time.

Thousands of these dolls have been made since 1872. However, they have now been discontinued by the Central Church's Society. As a result of this discontinuation, the value of the doll has been greatly enhanced.

The Moravian doll is 16" tall and is found dressed in either a pink and white or blue and white gingham dress covered by a white pinafore. The bonnet is matching with a row of lace sewn directly to the head. The faces are hand drawn and painted directly onto the fabric. All the faces vary greatly as each was done by a different individual. This tends to be a very soft-colored doll.

The Moravian is a difficult doll to find, especially the older versions.

Philadelphia or Sheppard Baby

Not a great deal is known about this elusive rag doll, except that it was made for the J.B. Sheppard Co. store of Philadelphia, Penn. around the turn of the century. It came in sizes 18" to 22" and is a rather well-made doll with a great deal of attention given to the facial features. It appears to have come dressed as either a girl or boy. The type of paint used on this doll was very thin with no apparent protective layer, therefore, it is very often found in poor condition having a lot of facial crackling.

Presbyterian Rag

The Presbyterian rag dolls were made in 1885 to raise money for the First Presbyterian Church of Bucyrus, Ohio. They were 17" tall, hand-painted with hand-sewn clothing of the period (ankle length dress with matching prairie bonnet). The appeal of the faces varies greatly according to the way in which they were painted.

In 1956, the dolls were once again made from the same pattern but using contemporary fabrics. These are easily differentiated from the old. Not an easy doll to find.

Rollinson

The Rollinson is very often mistaken for a Chase. The type of painting used and the body construction is very similar to that used by Chase.

This doll was designed by Gertrude F. Rollinson and manufactured by Utley Doll Co., Holyoke, Mass. from 1917 to 1919. The dolls came dressed or undressed, with painted hair or wigs, in sizes from 14" to 28". Because of their resemblance to Chase dolls, it is very helpful when these dolls still have their mark. It is found on the front of the torso stamped in a diamond shape, having a doll in the center and the words "Rollinson Doll, Holyoke, Mass." on the borders.

Izannah Walker

The Walker doll is said to have been the first patented rag doll in the United States. Mrs. Walker of Central Falls, R. I. patented her doll on Nov. 4, 1873, but is said to have begun making them around 1840. The early Izannah Walker doll is made entirely of cloth having the head and limbs painted thinly in oils. They ranged in size from 15" to 24". The bodies are found stuffed with cotton, horsehair, rags, or paper. Each has a very distinct look, as the faces came in many different styles and shapes. The hair also came painted in different styles; some had long curls, some had short brush stroke hair and some just swirls. The early dolls had applied ears and came with painted boots or barefooted.

The later patented dolls were somewhat different in construction. The heads were separate. The ears were molded, and the facial features lacked definition. They also all had the painted shoes. The clothes they wore were those of the period, most well-known is the off-the-shoulder dress.

The Walker doll is not a particularly pretty doll, but it is the most greatly treasured rag doll, not to mention the most expensive.

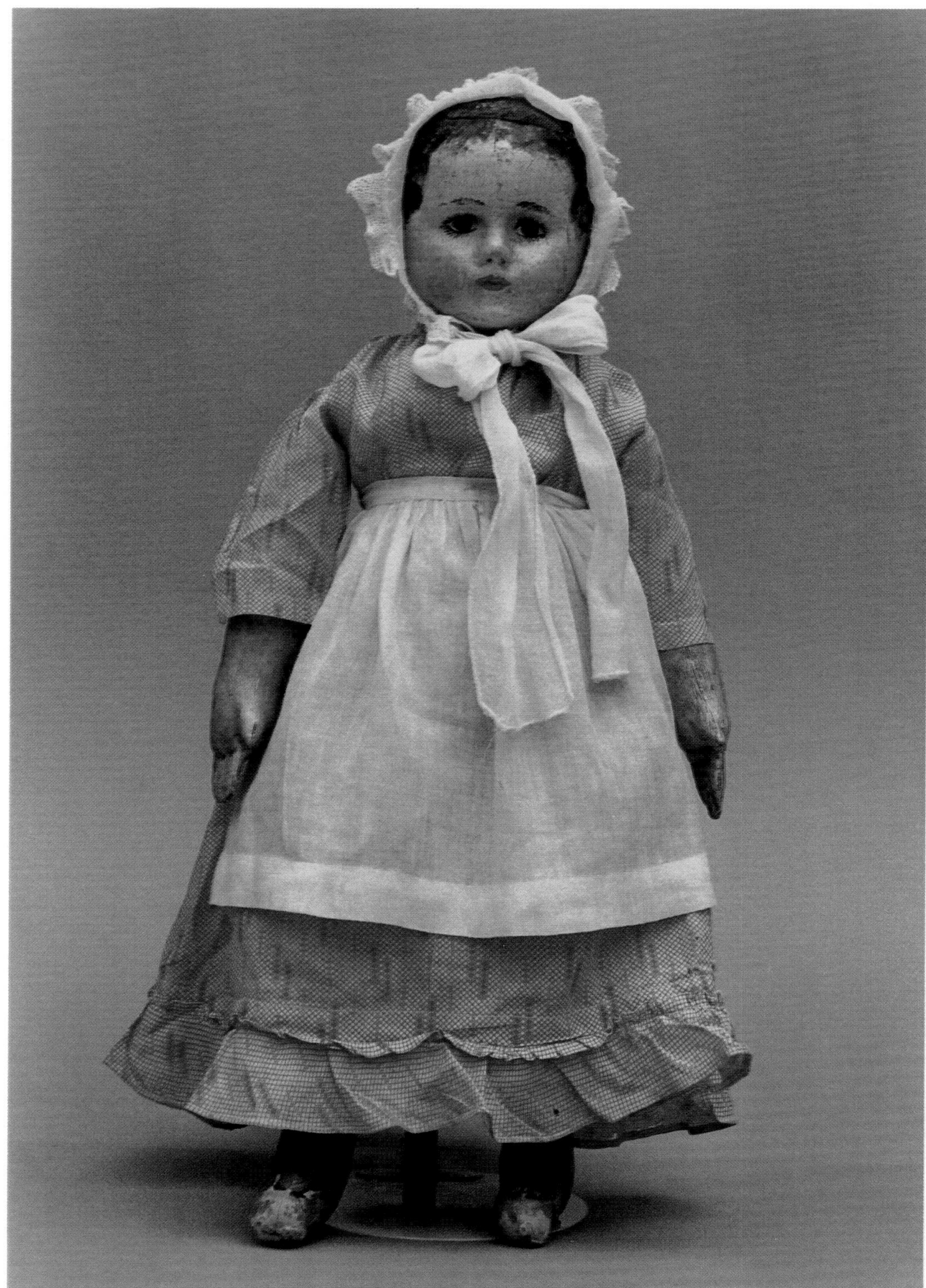

Collection of Mary Worrow

Type: 22" Early Alabama Baby
Construction: *Body* - hard stuffed with painted extremeties; jointed at hips and shoulders; short painted shoes; *Head* - applied sewn-on pate; applied ears; *Clothes* - old, not original
Clues to Dating: marked on lower torso: patent no. 2

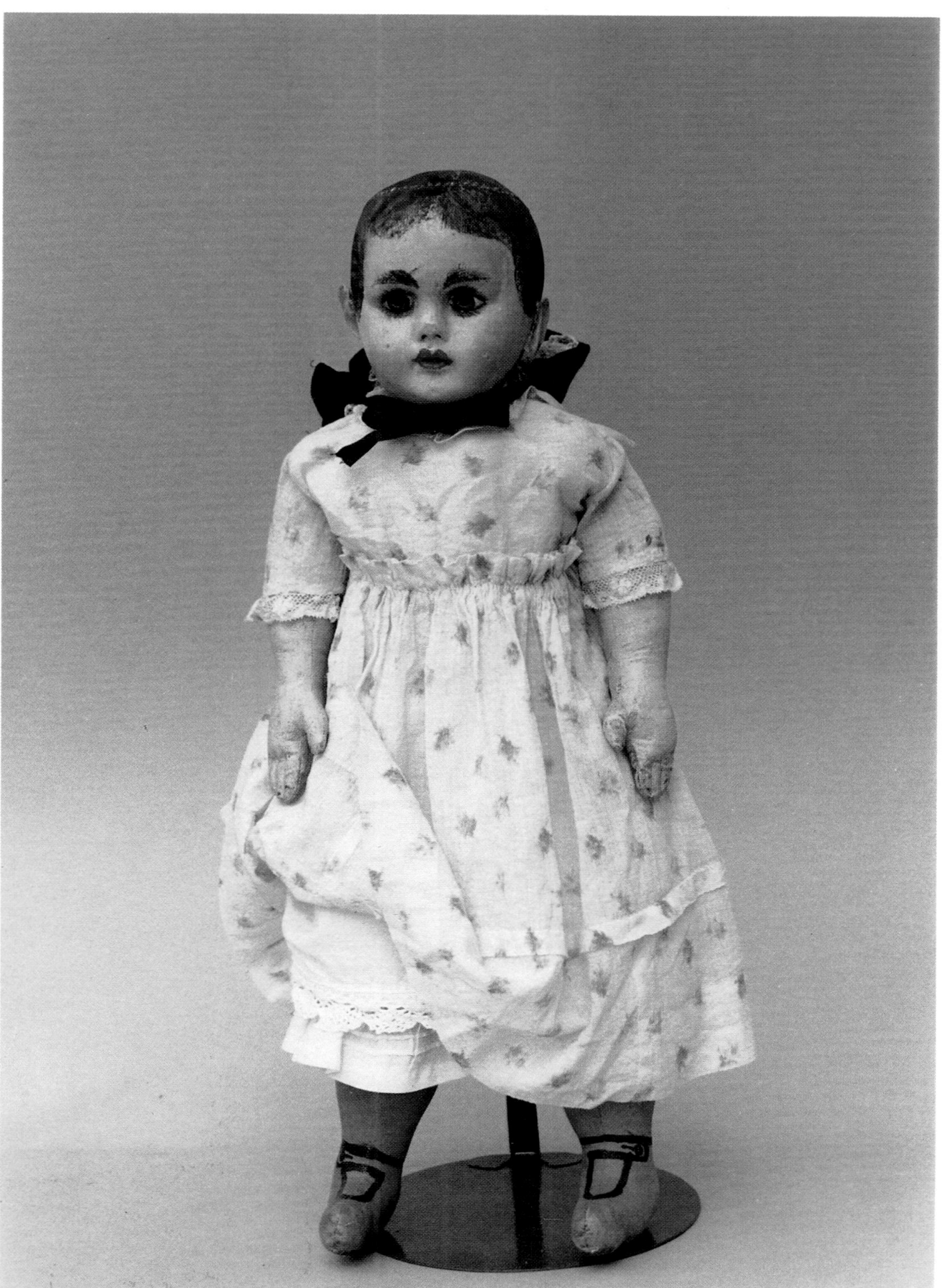

Author's Collection

Type: 22'' Early Alabama Baby
Construction: *Body* - hard stuffed with painted extremeties; jointed at hips and shoulders; boots painted to top of leg; *Head* - sewn-on pate and applied ears; *Clothes* - old, not original
Clues to Dating: marked on lower torso

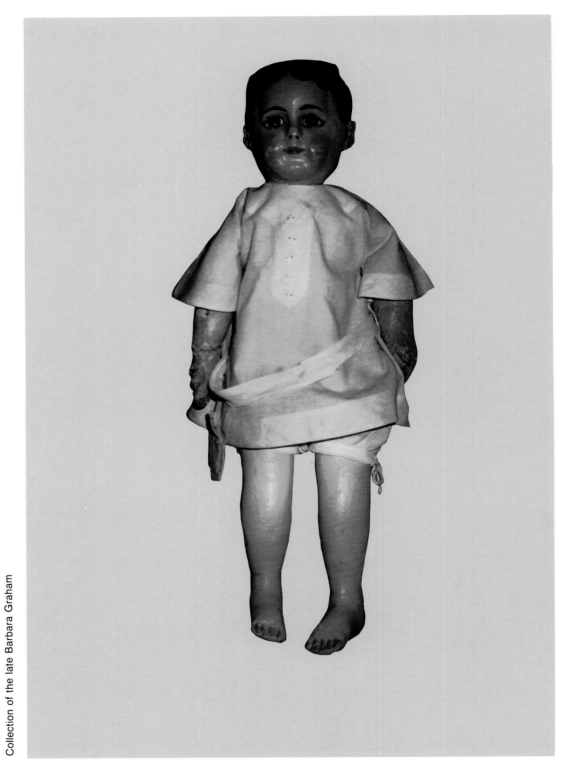
Collection of the late Barbara Graham

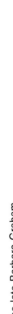

Type: 24" Barefoot Alabama Baby
Construction: *Body* - same as previous dolls except for the bare feet with stitched toes; *Clothes* - old

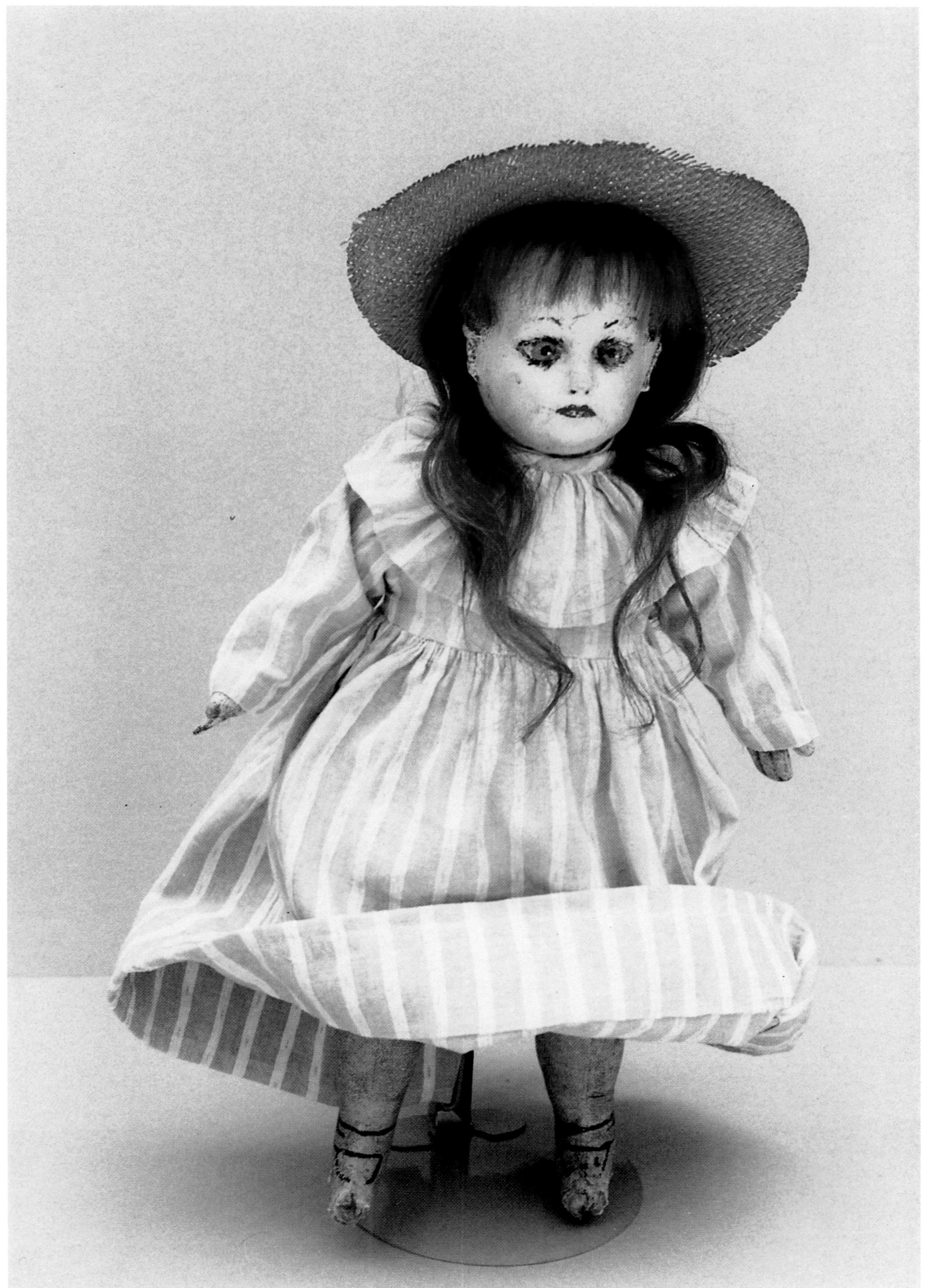

Author's Collection

Type: 14" Alabama Baby With Wig
Construction: *Body* - cloth hard stuffed with cotton fingers stitched, thumbs separate; arms painted; has blue painted boots; jointed at shoulders and hips; *Features* - molded and painted; ears applied; *Hair* - human hair wig; *Clothes* - old

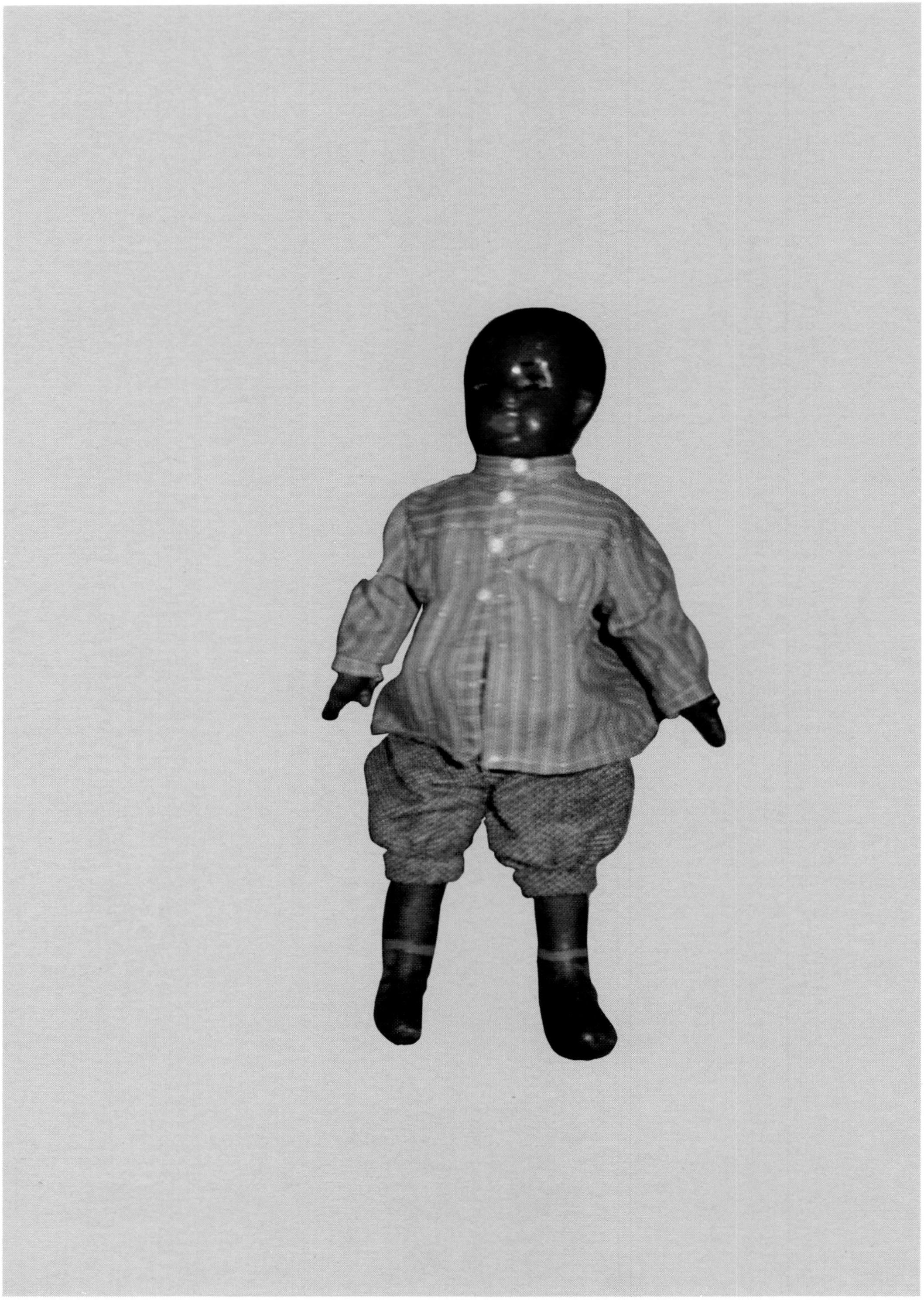

Collection of the late Barbara Graham

Type: 14" Rare Black Alabama Baby
Construction: *Body* - brown muslin fabric; head does not have pate, but is made in two pieces with molded ears not applied; *Limbs* - painted brown high top boots; *Clothes* - old

Collection of Mary Worrow

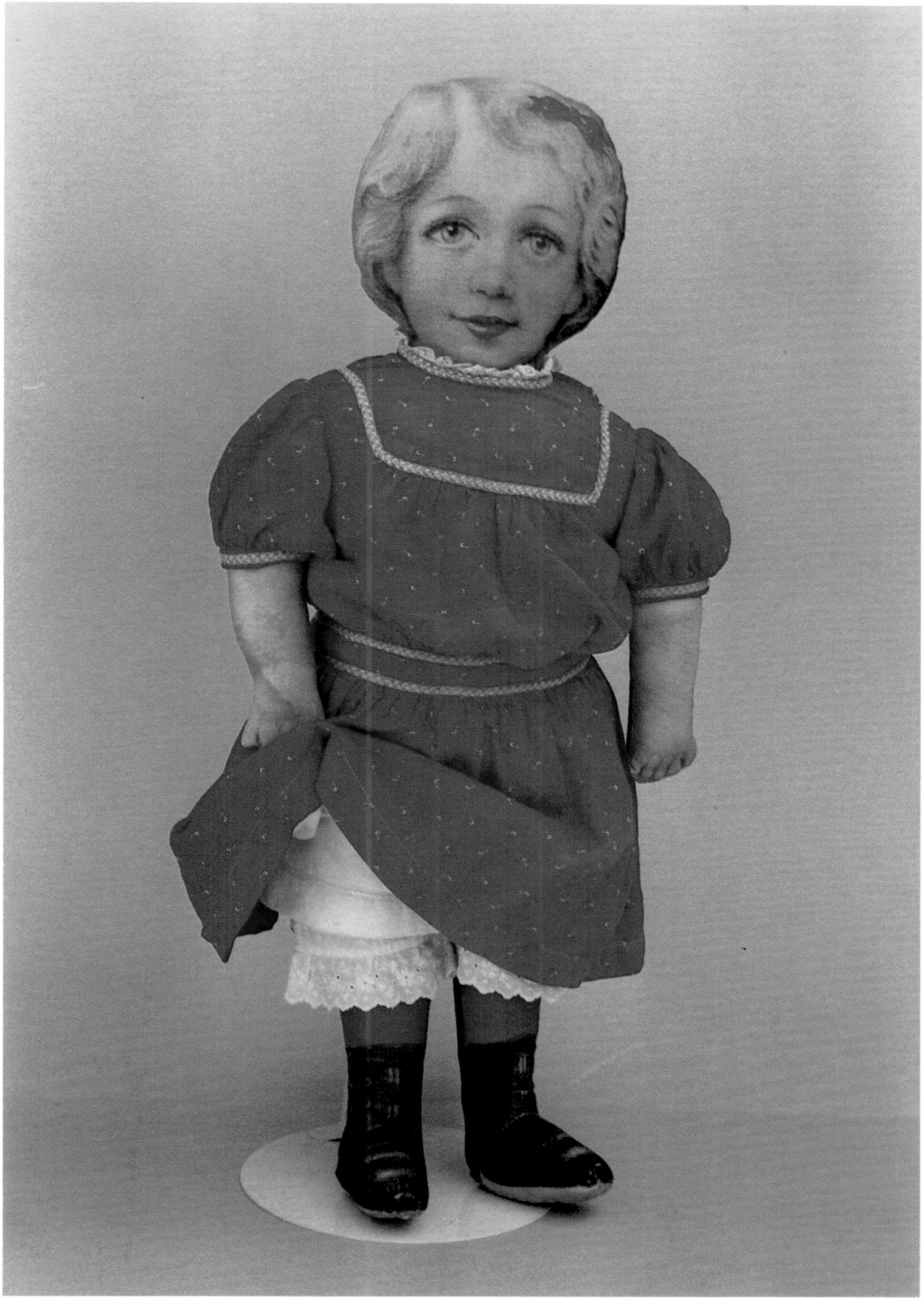

Type: 26" Art Fabric Girl
Construction: *Body* - lithograph on heavy muslin; colors very vibrant; not jointed; stuffed with cotton; *Clothes* - old

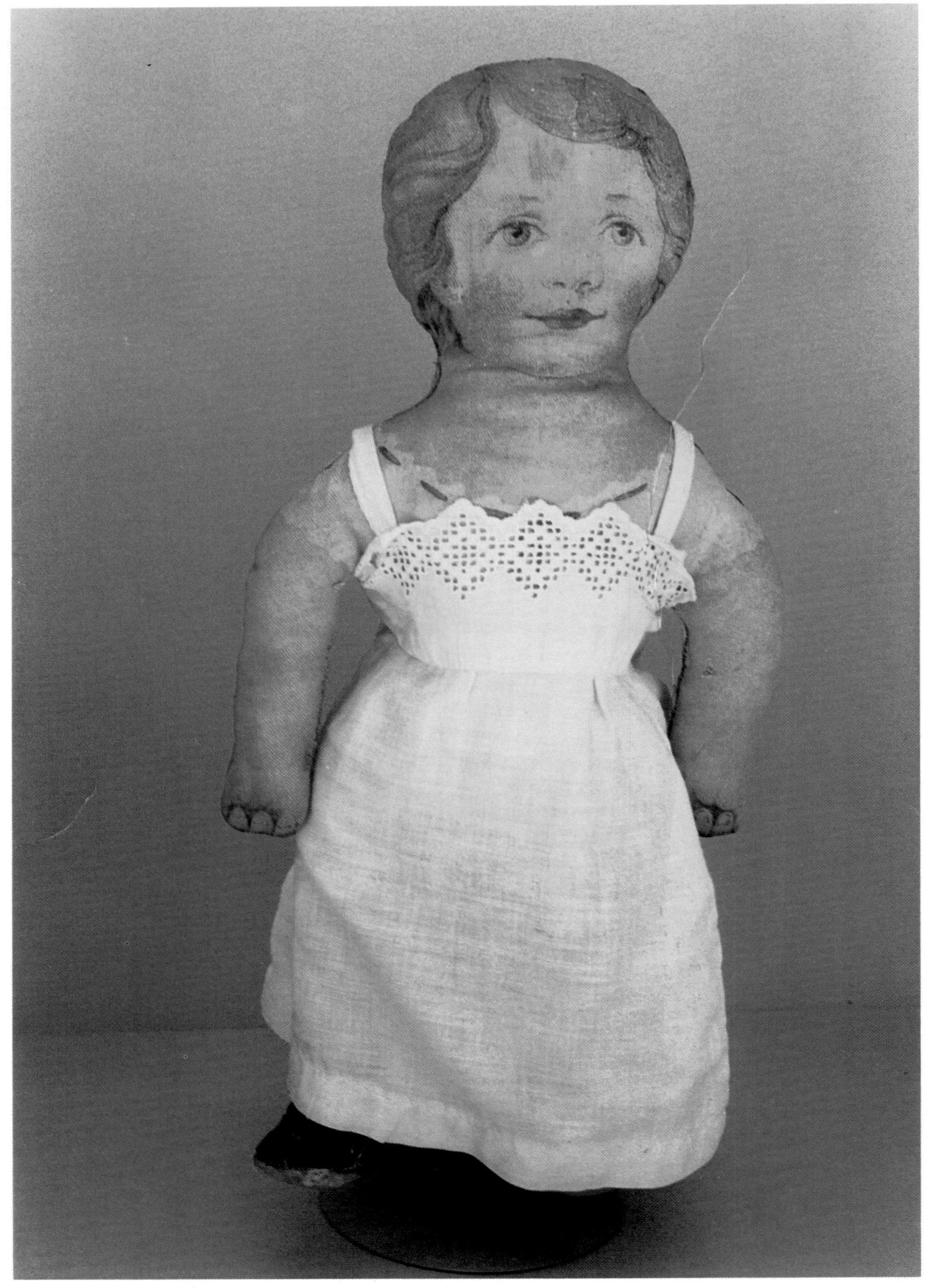

Type: 26" Art Fabric Girl
Construction: *Body* - lithograph on heavy muslin; not jointed; stuffed with cotton; marked under foot; *Clothes* - old

Collection of Charlene Lucinian

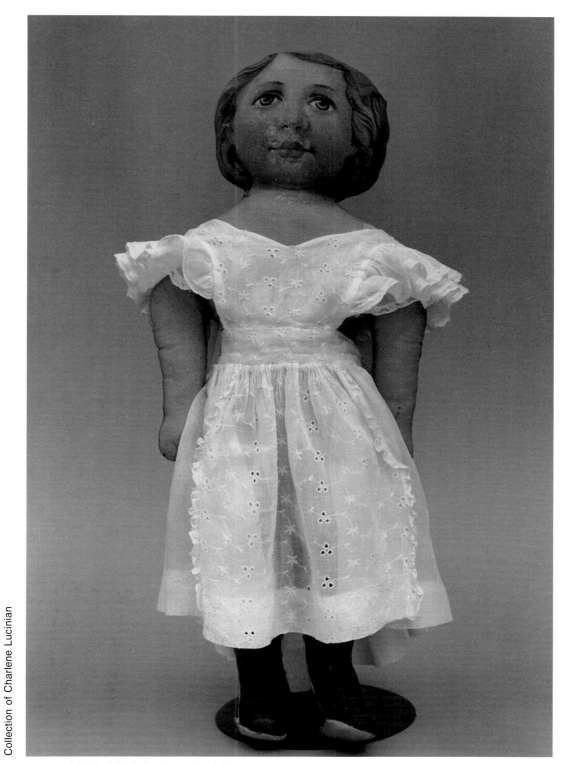

Type: 16" Art Fabric Circa 1900s
Construction: *Body* - muslin stuffed with old cotton; *Features* - lithographed

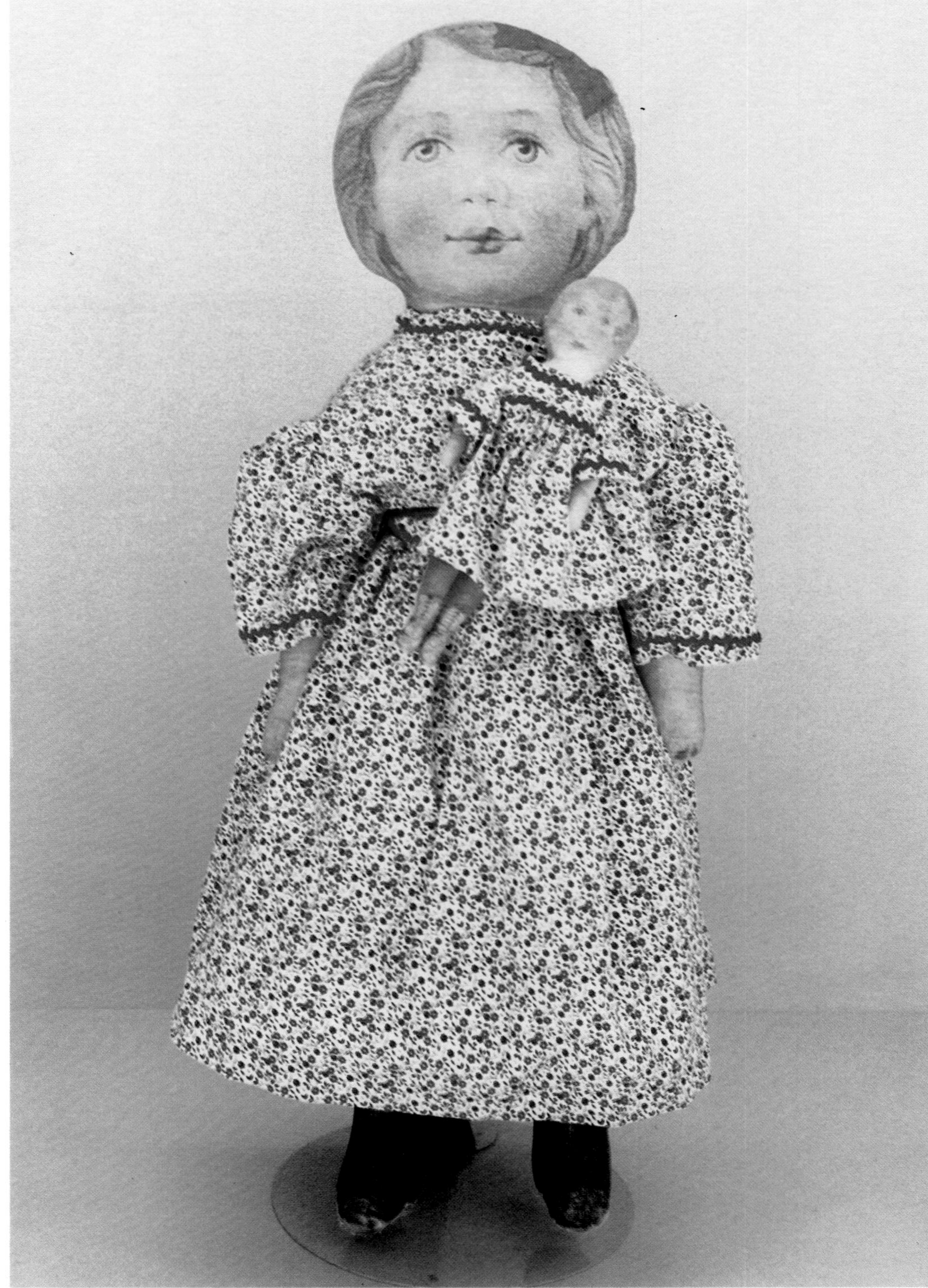

Collection of Charlene Lucinian

Type: 25" and 8" Art Fabric Dolls
Construction: *Body* - muslin stuffed with straw; *Features* - lithographed; *Clothes* - new

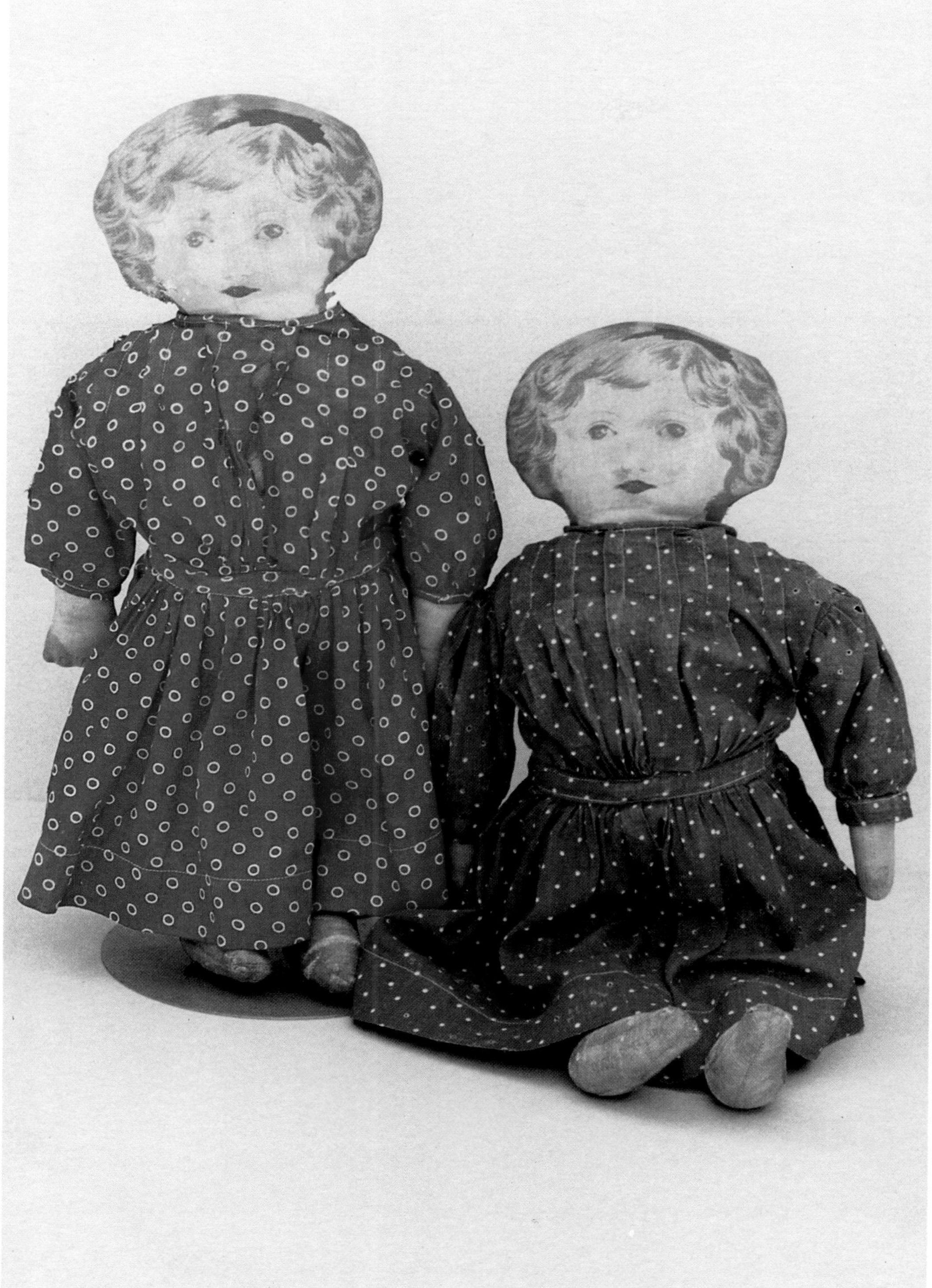

Collection of Charlene Lucinian

Type: 18" Twin Art Fabric Dolls
Construction: *Body* - muslin stuffed with cotton; *Features* - lithographed; *Clothes* - dresses are original to the dolls

♥

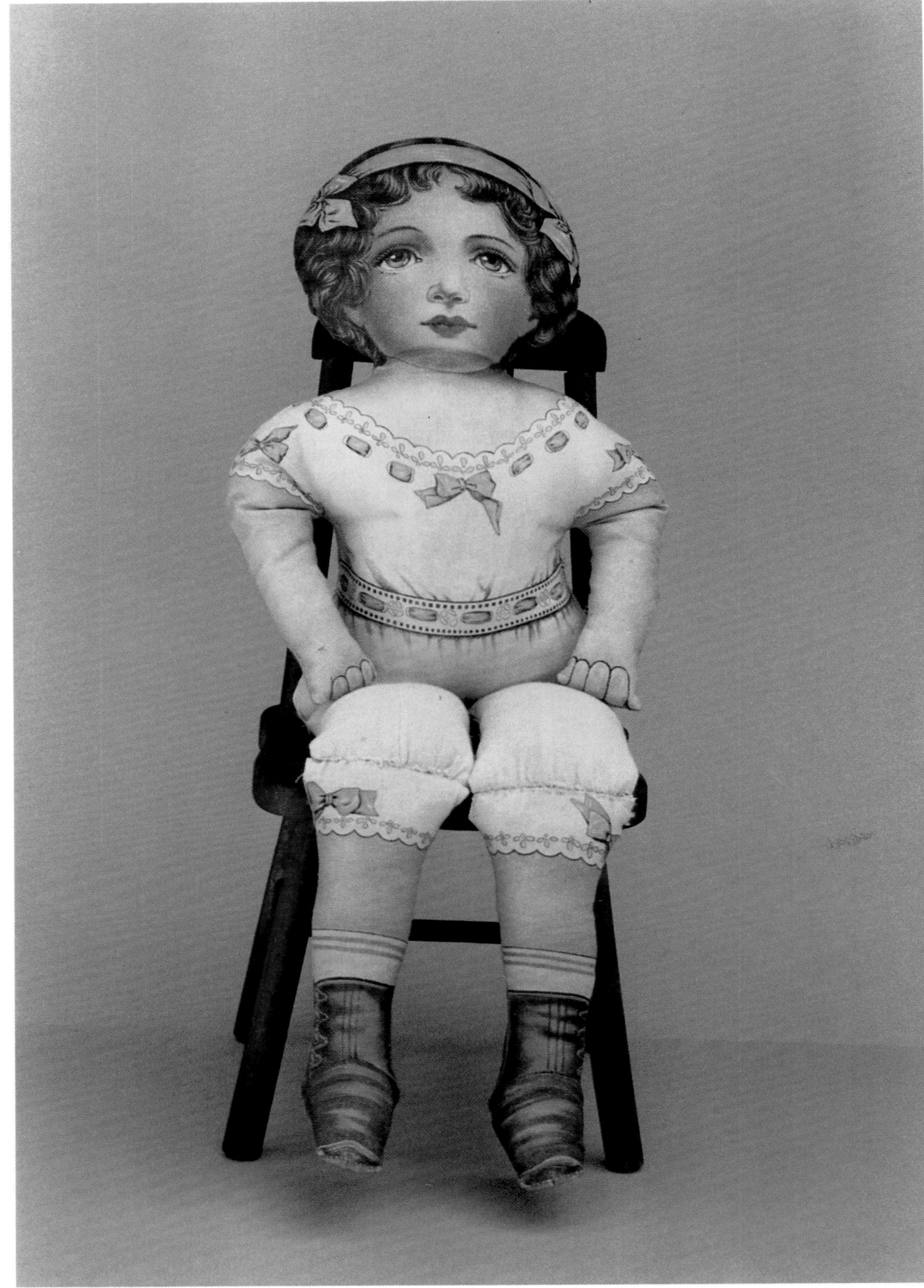

Collection of Mary Worrow

Type: 30" Art Fabric Merrie Marie
Construction: *Body* - lithograph on heavy cotton; stuffed with cotton; joints made at the knees

Author's Collection

Type: 10" and 12" Lithographed Children attributed to Horsman Co. circa 1903
Construction: *Body* - cotton printed fabric stuffed with cotton

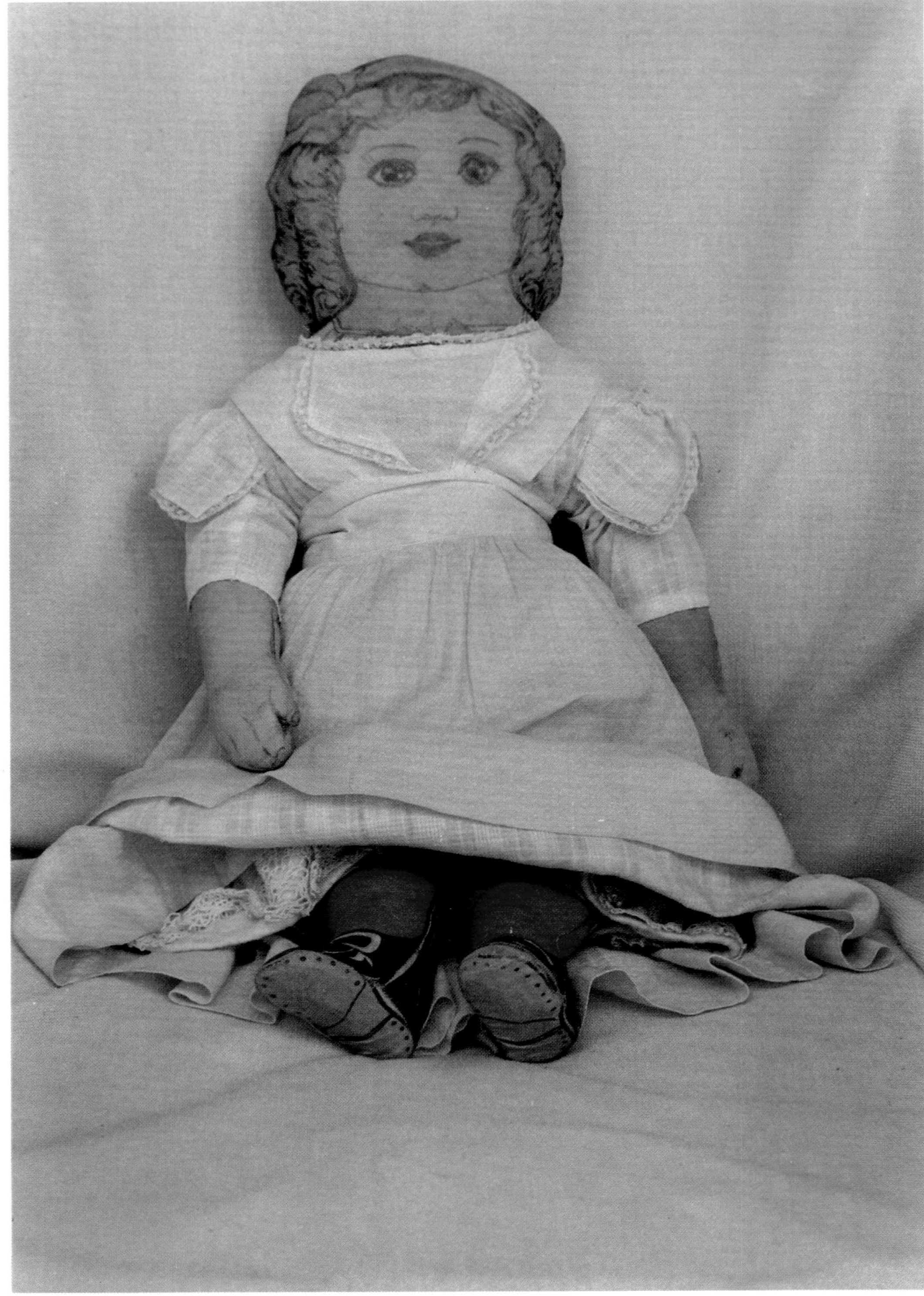

Collection of Margie Kimbro

Type: 26" Lithograph Girl Circa 1900s
Construction: *Body* - cotton printed fabric stuffed with cotton; *Clothes* - old

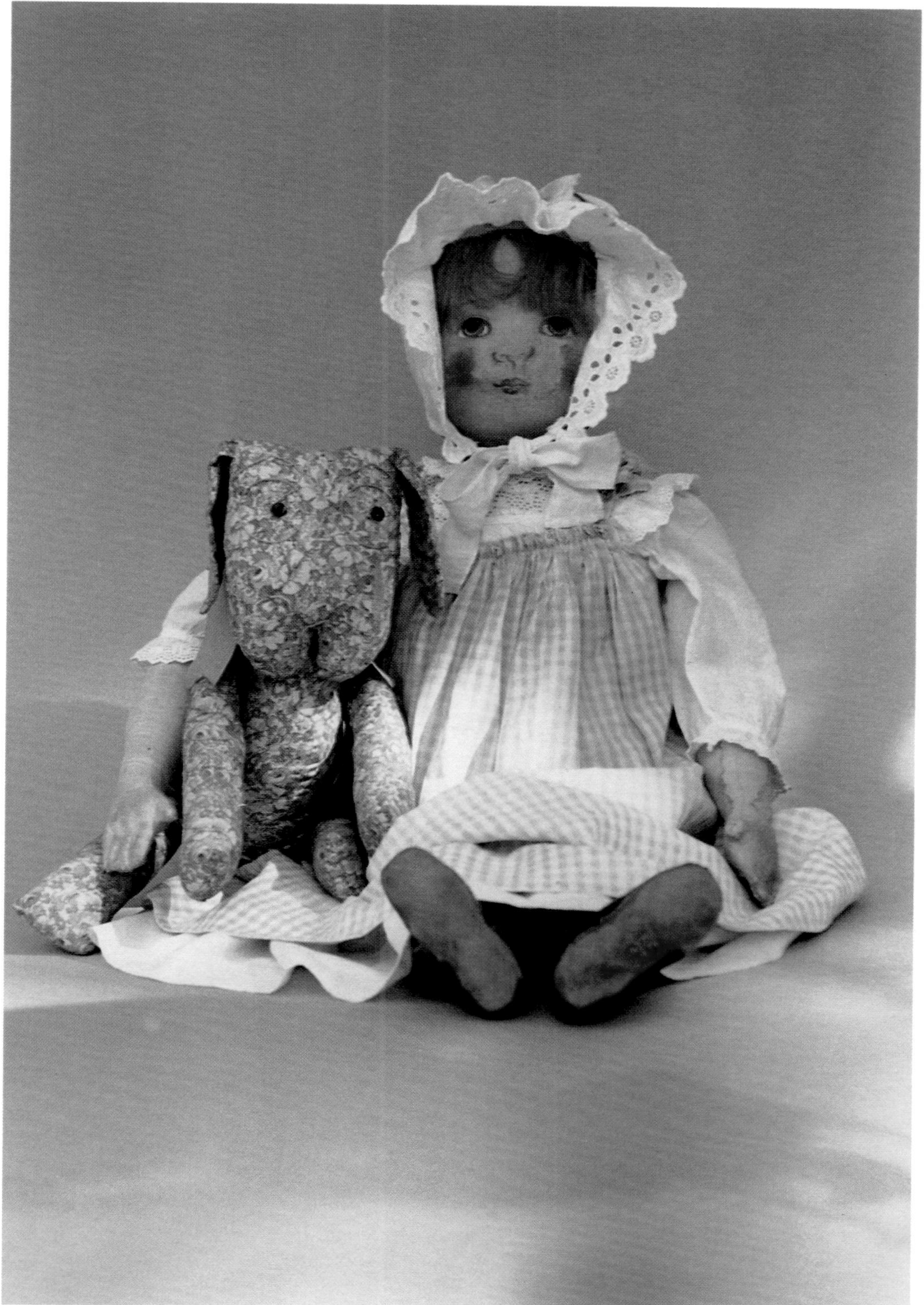

Author's Collection

Type: 30" Early Babyland
Construction: *Hands* - stitched fingers; elbows jointed; *Features* - painted; original hair; *Clothes* - not original, but old and a good likeness

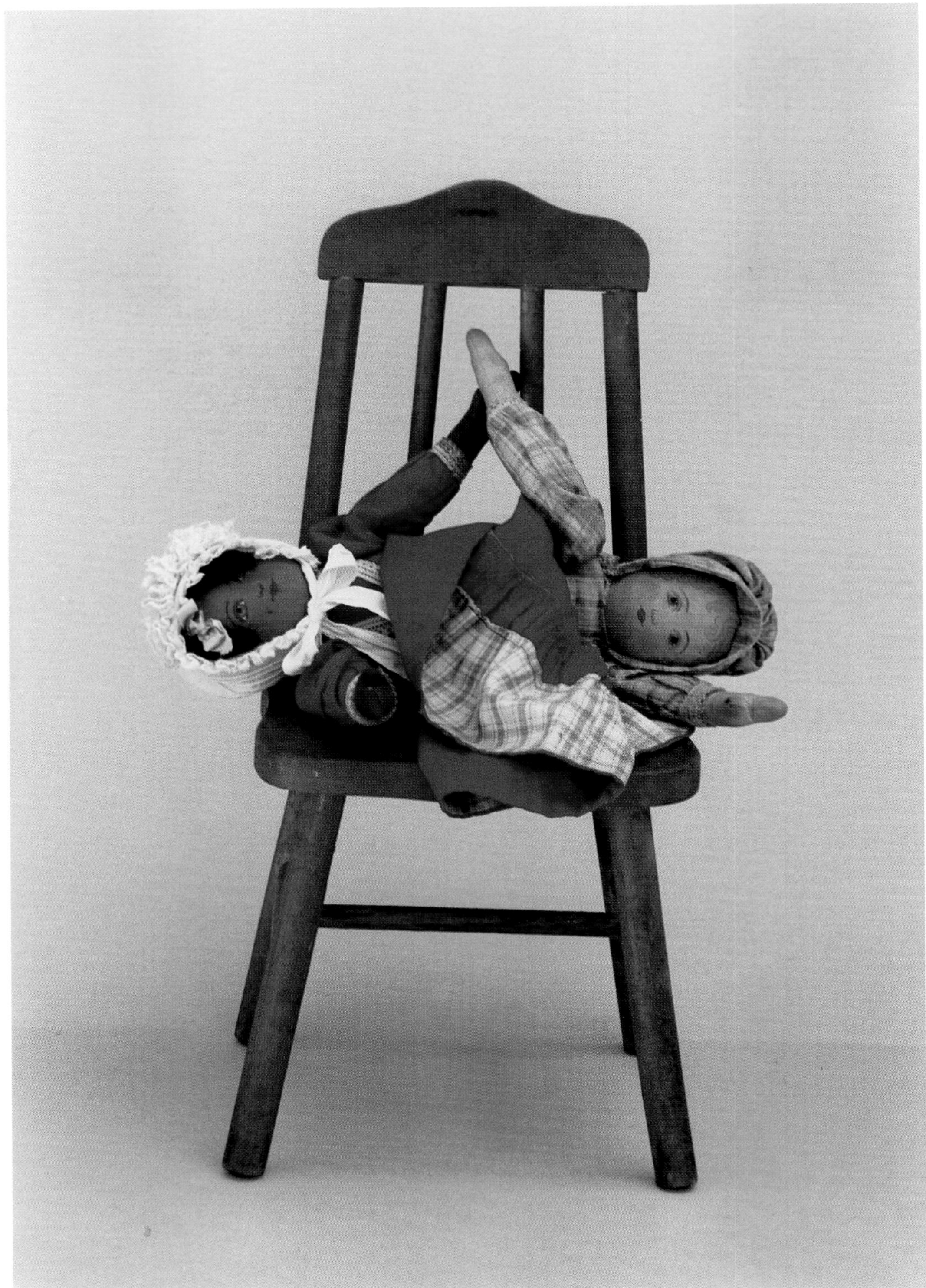

Collection of Mary Worrow

Type: 12'' Early Topsy-Turvy Babyland
Construction: *Body* - hard stuffed muslin; *Hands* - mitts; *Features* - painted; black side has mohair wig; *Clothes* - original

Collection of Jim and Phyllis Youtz

Type: 23'' White Beecher
Construction: *Body* - needle sculpted pink stockingnette; stitched fingers and toes; jointed at knees, hips and shoulders; *Features* - needle sculpted and painted; sparse wool yarn hair; *Clothes* - old, not original

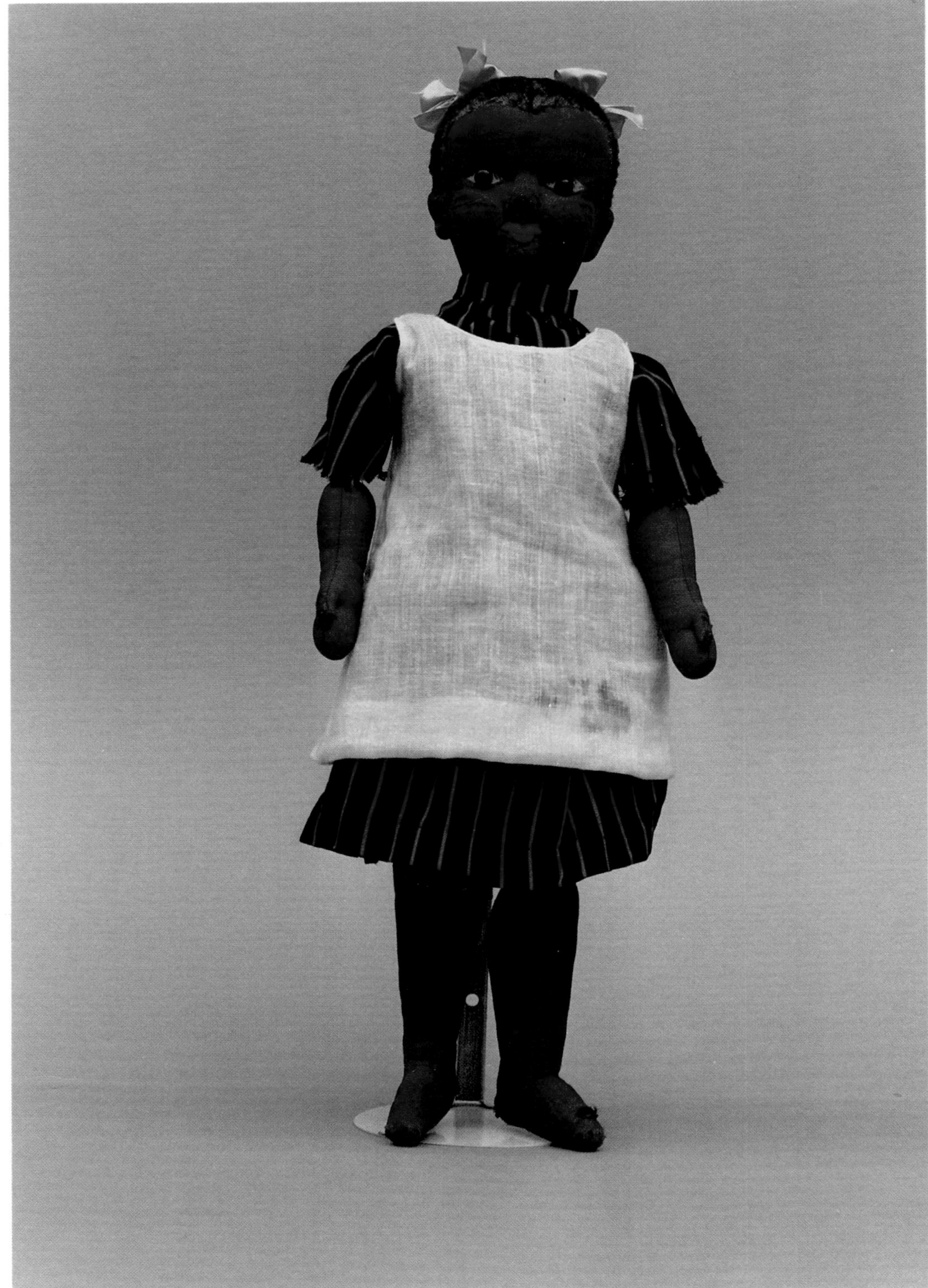

Collection of Mary Worrow

Type: 18'' Black Beecher Type
Construction: *Body* - soft black sateen; jointed at the knees; *Hands* - mitts; *Feet* - stubs; *Features* - molded and stitched; wool hair; *Clothes* - dress and underclothes are original to the doll

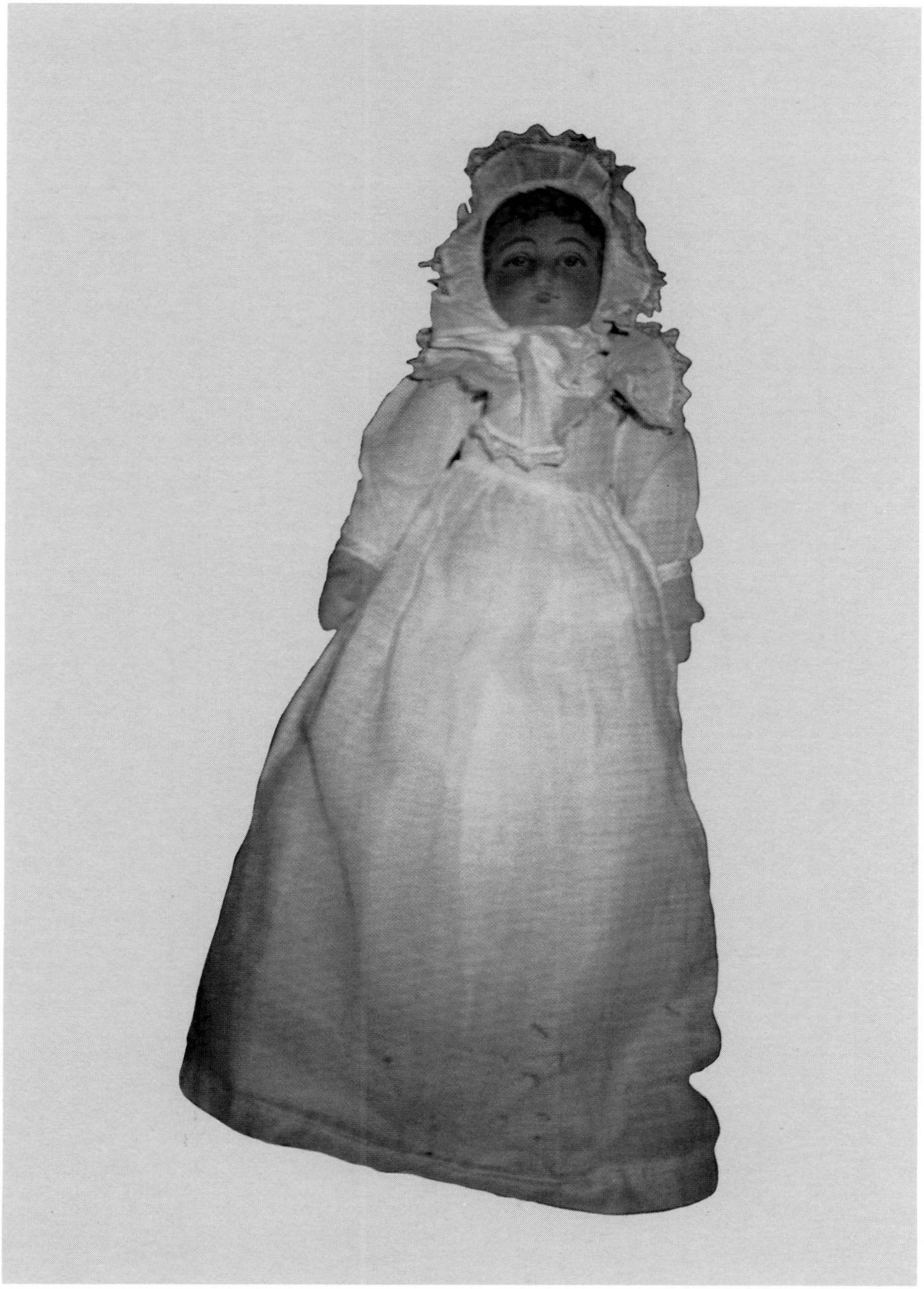

Collection of the late Barbara Graham

Type: 14'' Baby Bruckner Rag Doll
Construction: *Body* - same as following doll, except for the feet which are stubs; *Clothes* - all original

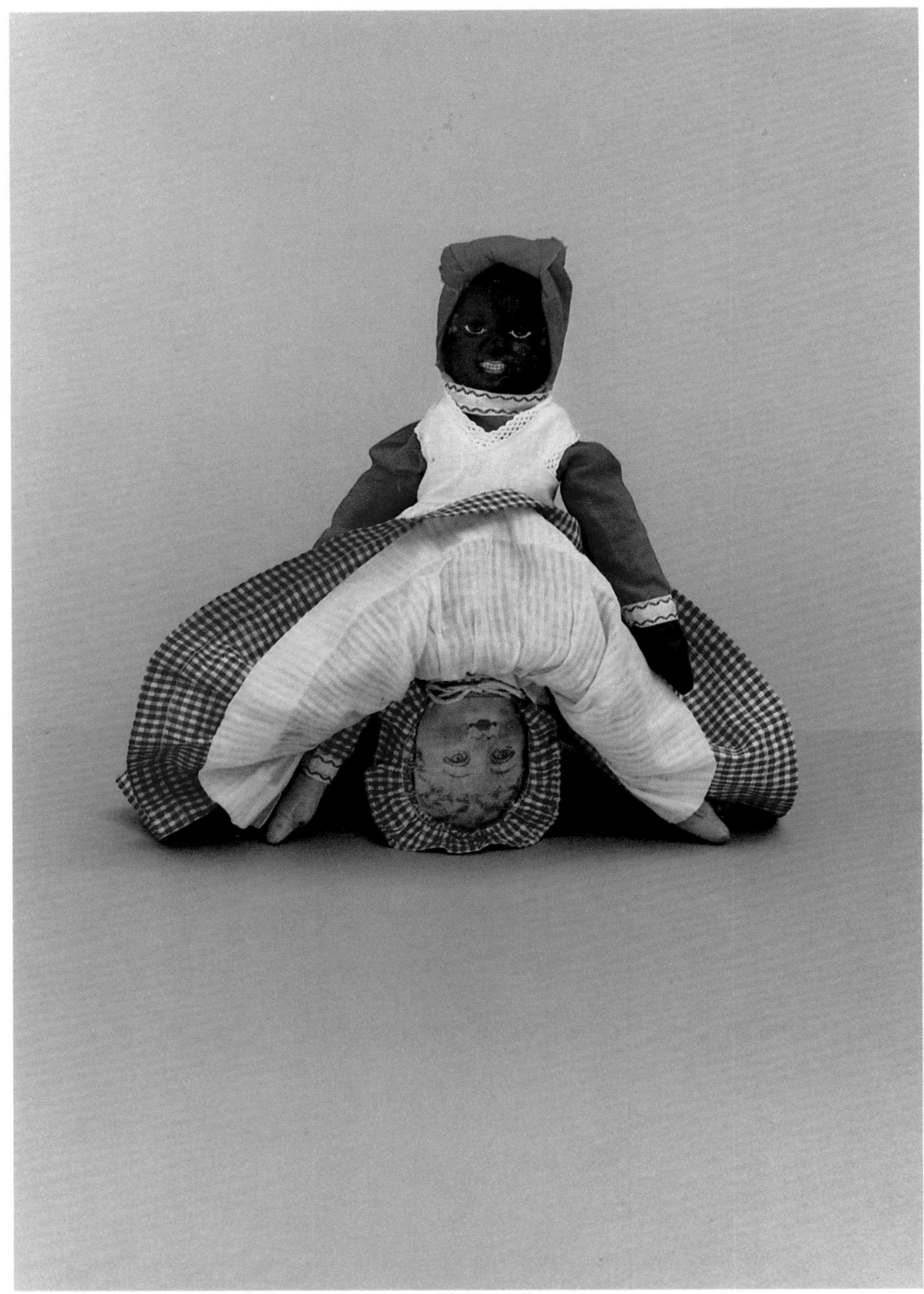

Collection of Mary Worrow

Type: 12'' Topsy-Turvy Bruckner
Construction: *Body* - stuffed with cotton; *Hands* - mitts; *Features* - painted upon a mask; *Clothes* - original

Author's Collection

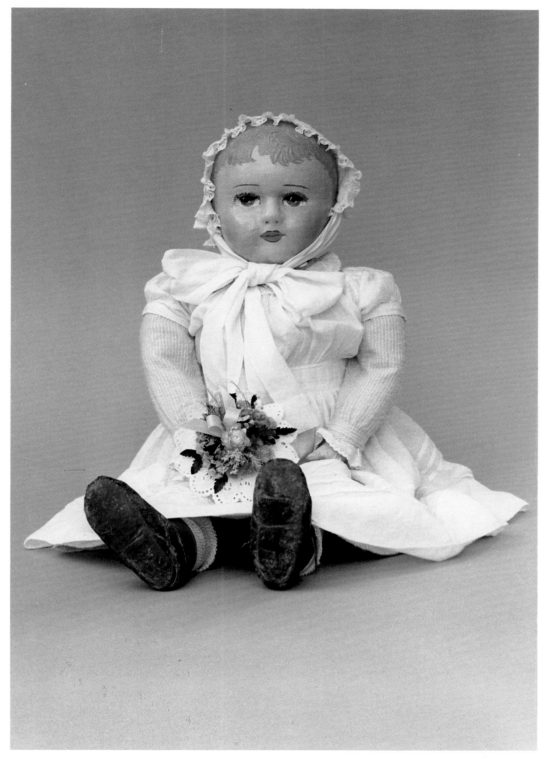

Type: 27'' Early Chase Child Doll

Construction: *Body* - pink sateen stuffed with cotton; jointed at knees, elbows, hips and shoulders; arms and legs are partially painted; *Features* - molded and heavily painted; ears are applied; mark stamped on lower hip; *Clothes* - old, not original

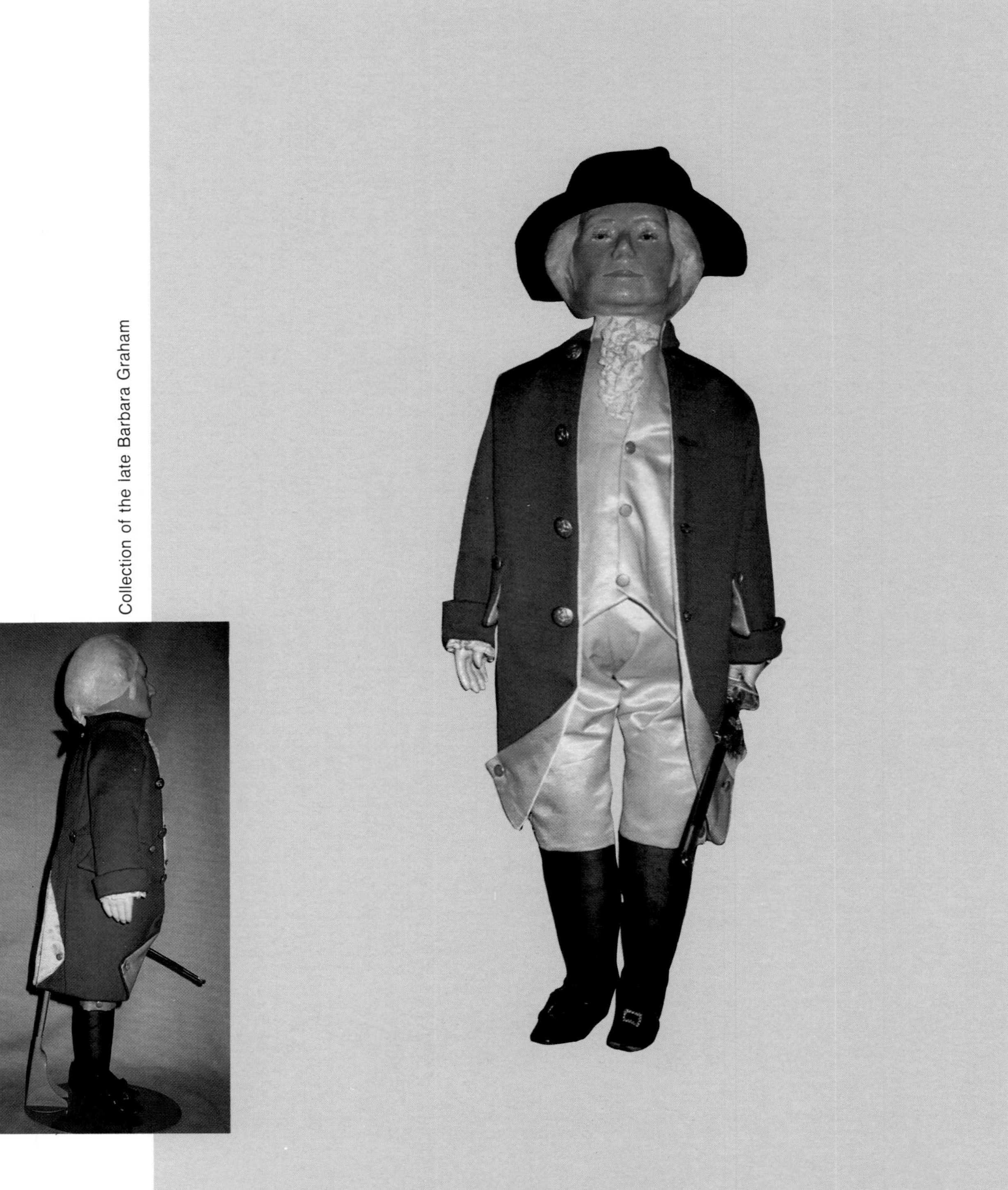

Collection of the late Barbara Graham

Type: 25'' Chase George Washington
Construction: *Body* - molded painted features and hair; jointed at shoulders and hips; all original

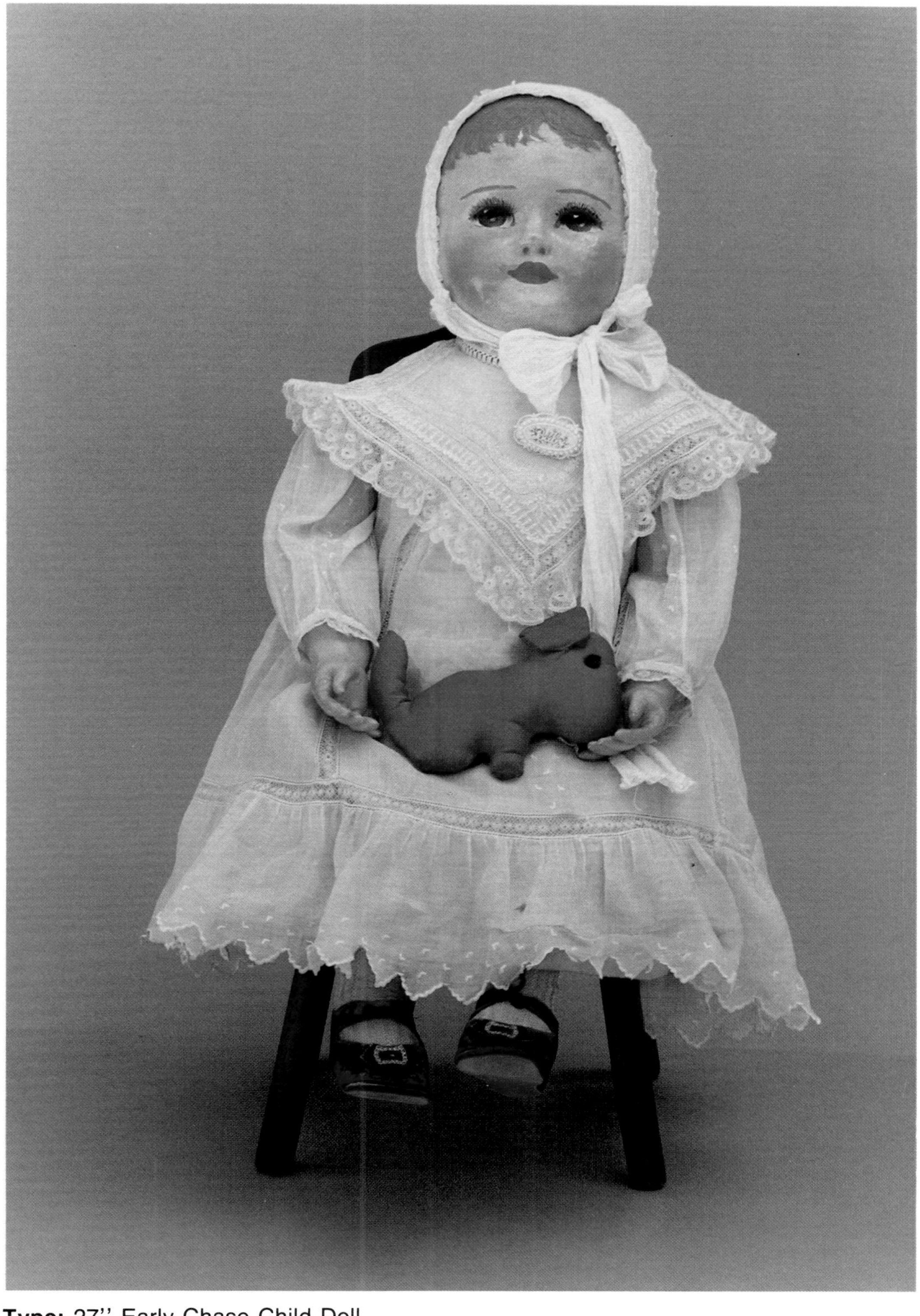

Collection of Mary Worrow

Type: 27" Early Chase Child Doll
Construction: *Body* - pink sateen stuffed with cotton; jointed at knees, elbows, hips and shoulders; arms and legs are partially painted; *Features* - molded and heavily painted; ears are applied; mark stamped on lower hip; *Clothes* - old, not original

Collection of Caroline Edleman

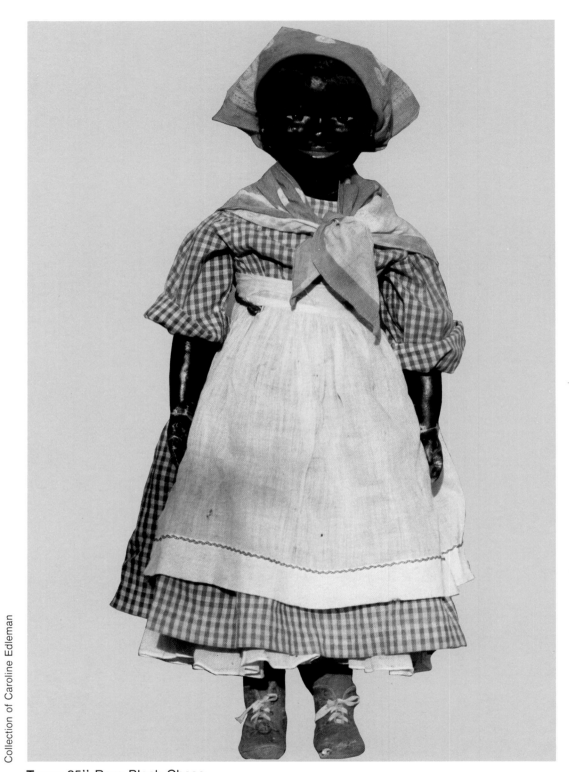

Type: 25" Rare Black Chase
Construction: *Body* - black cloth; arms and legs are painted; *Features* - ethnic, molded and painted; painted hair; *Clothes* - old

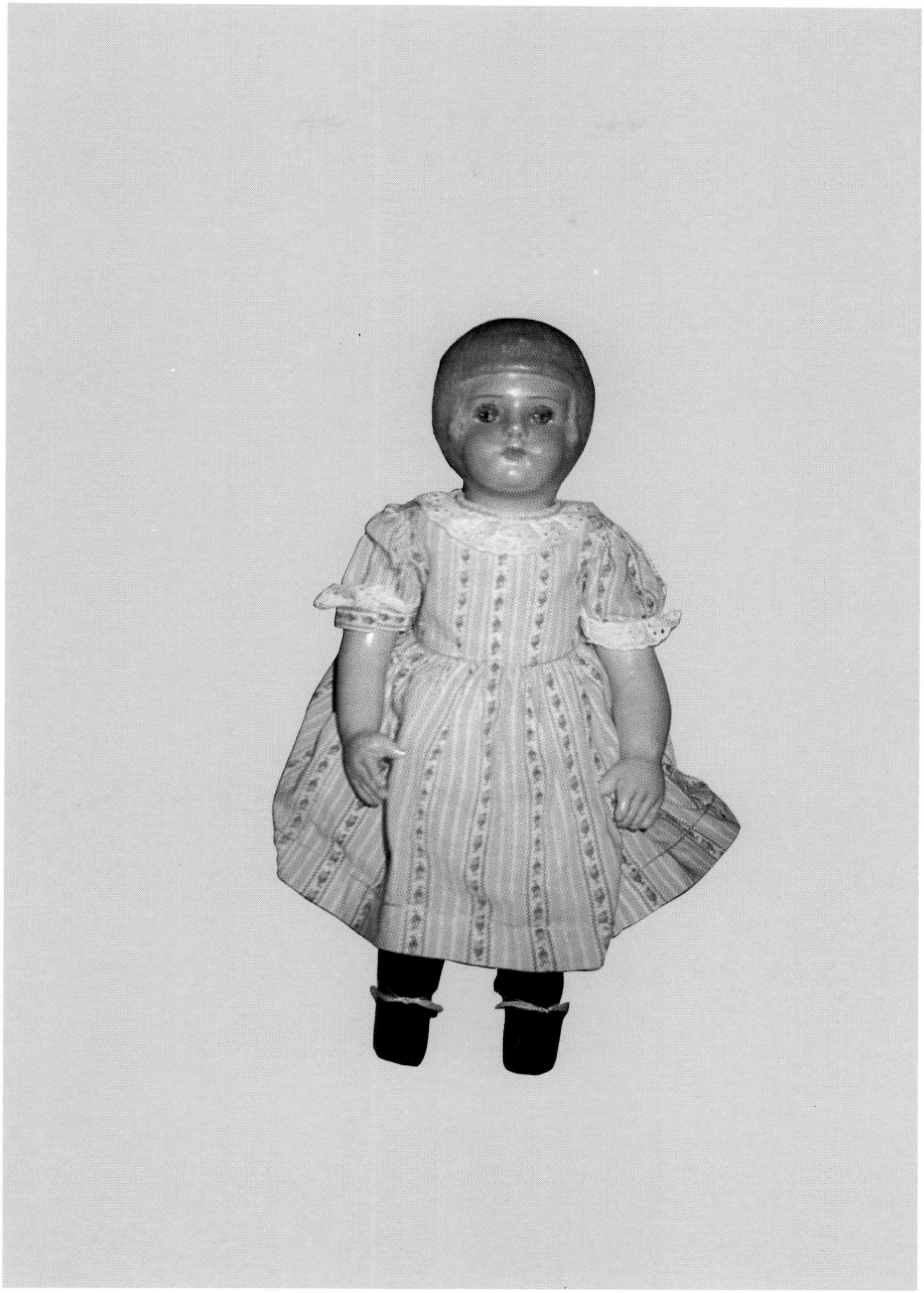

Collection of the late Barbara Graham

Type: 16" Chase Girl with Bobbed Hair
Construction: *Body* - fully painted, including limbs; jointed; *Hair* - molded in a bob; *Clothes* - contemporary

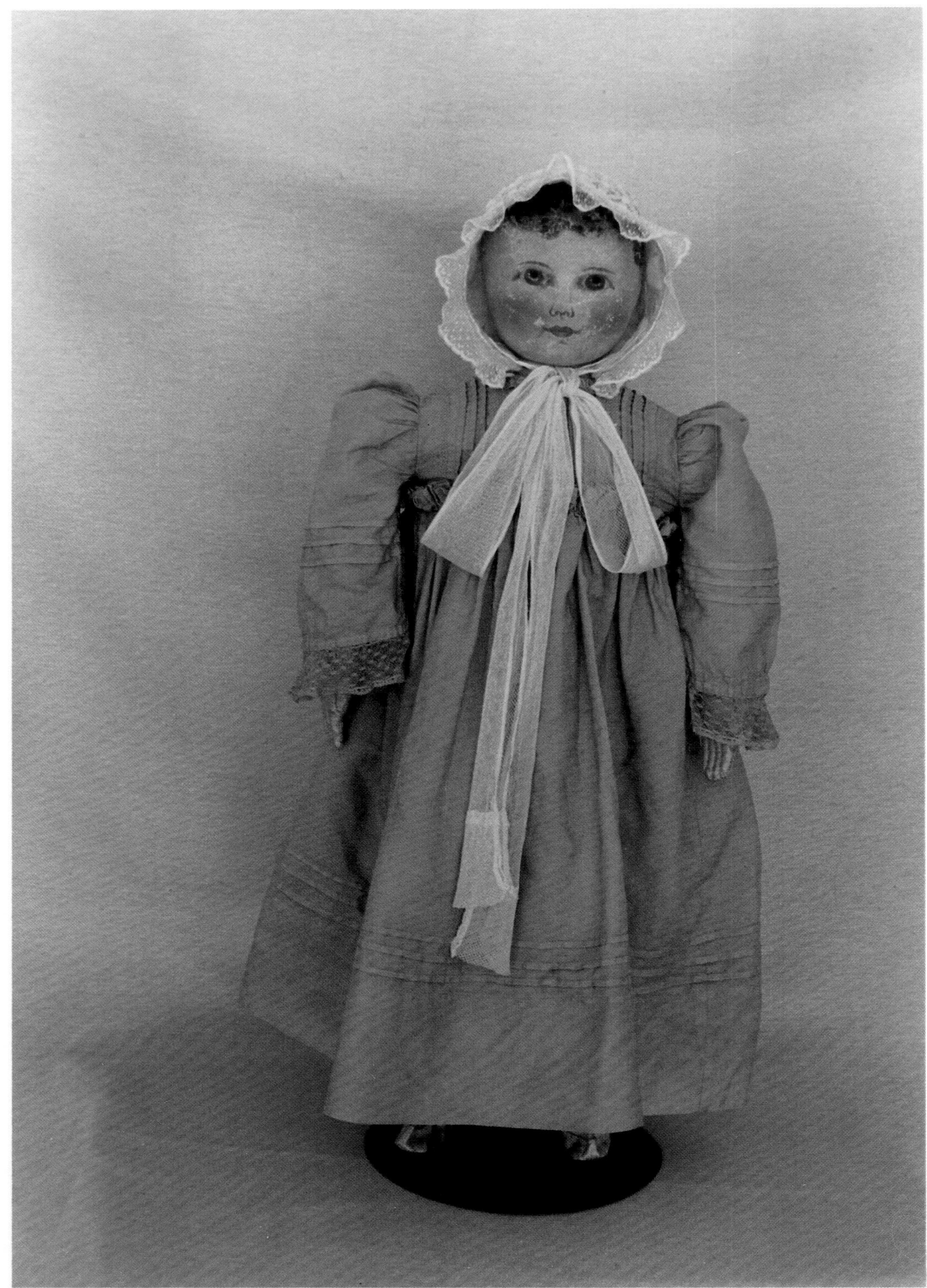

Author's Collection

Type: 23'' Columbian
Construction: *Body* - heavy cotton jointed at knees, hips and shoulders; *Hands* - stitched fingers with free standing thumbs; *Feet* - toes are stitched; arms and legs are painted mid-way to the top; *Features* - oilpainted; the curly-Q type nose is attributed to Emma Adams; the straight type nose is said to have been done by the employed artists; this doll is the straight nose version; *Clothes* - dress may be original

Collection of Mary Worrow

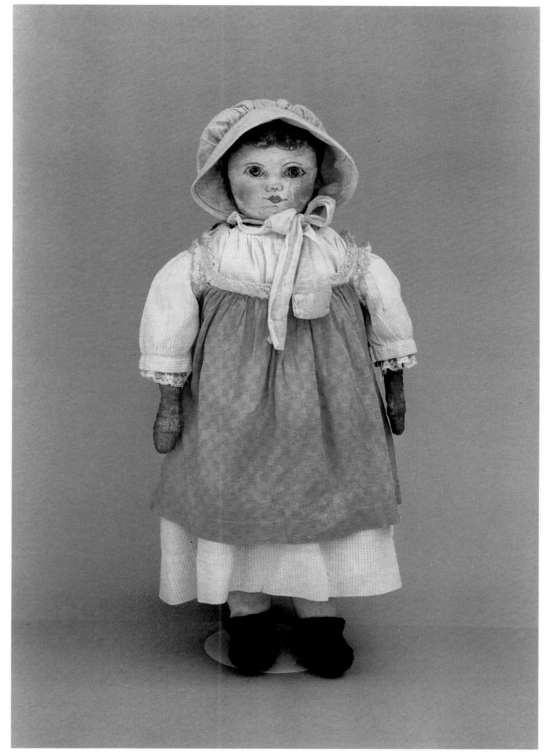

Type: 19'' Columbian

Construction: *Body* - same as previous doll pictured, except this one has the more often found curly-Q type nose; *Clothes* - not original, but old and appropriate

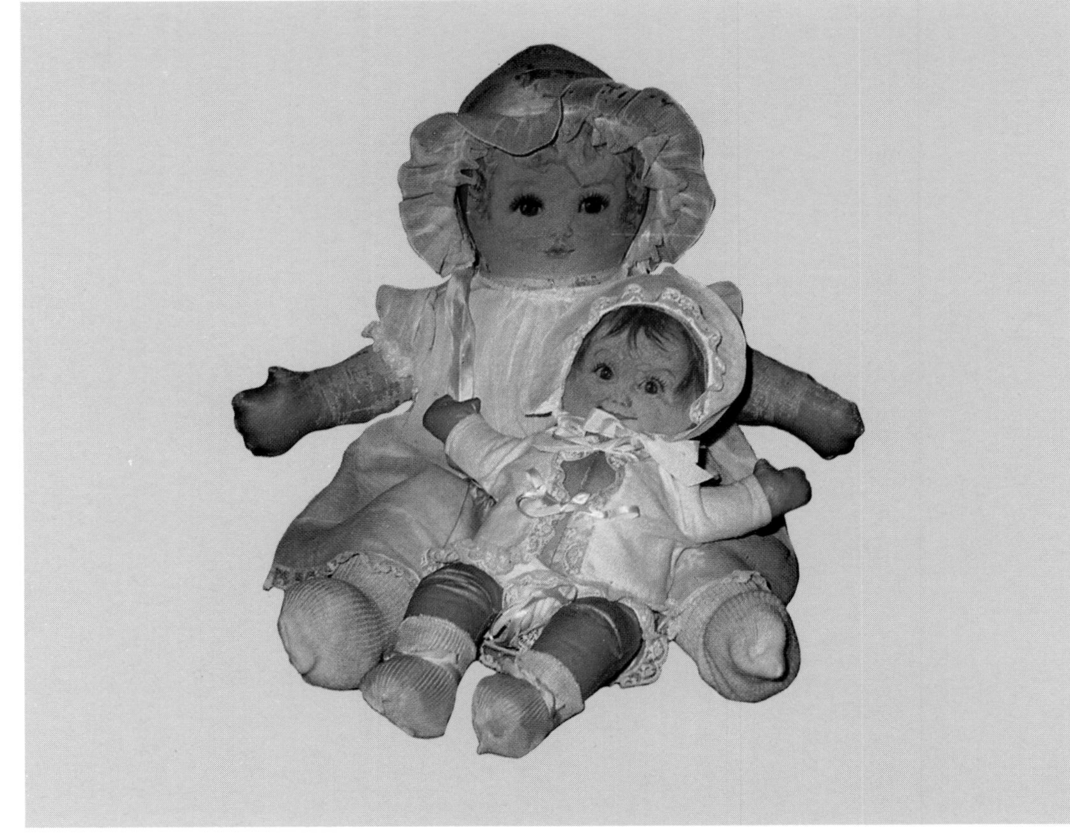

Collection of the late Barbara Graham

Type: 24" Sweets and 14" Baby by Maude Tausy Fangle
Construction: *Body* - cotton bodies stuffed with cotton; both jointed at shoulders and hips; *Features* - printed; *Clothes* - original

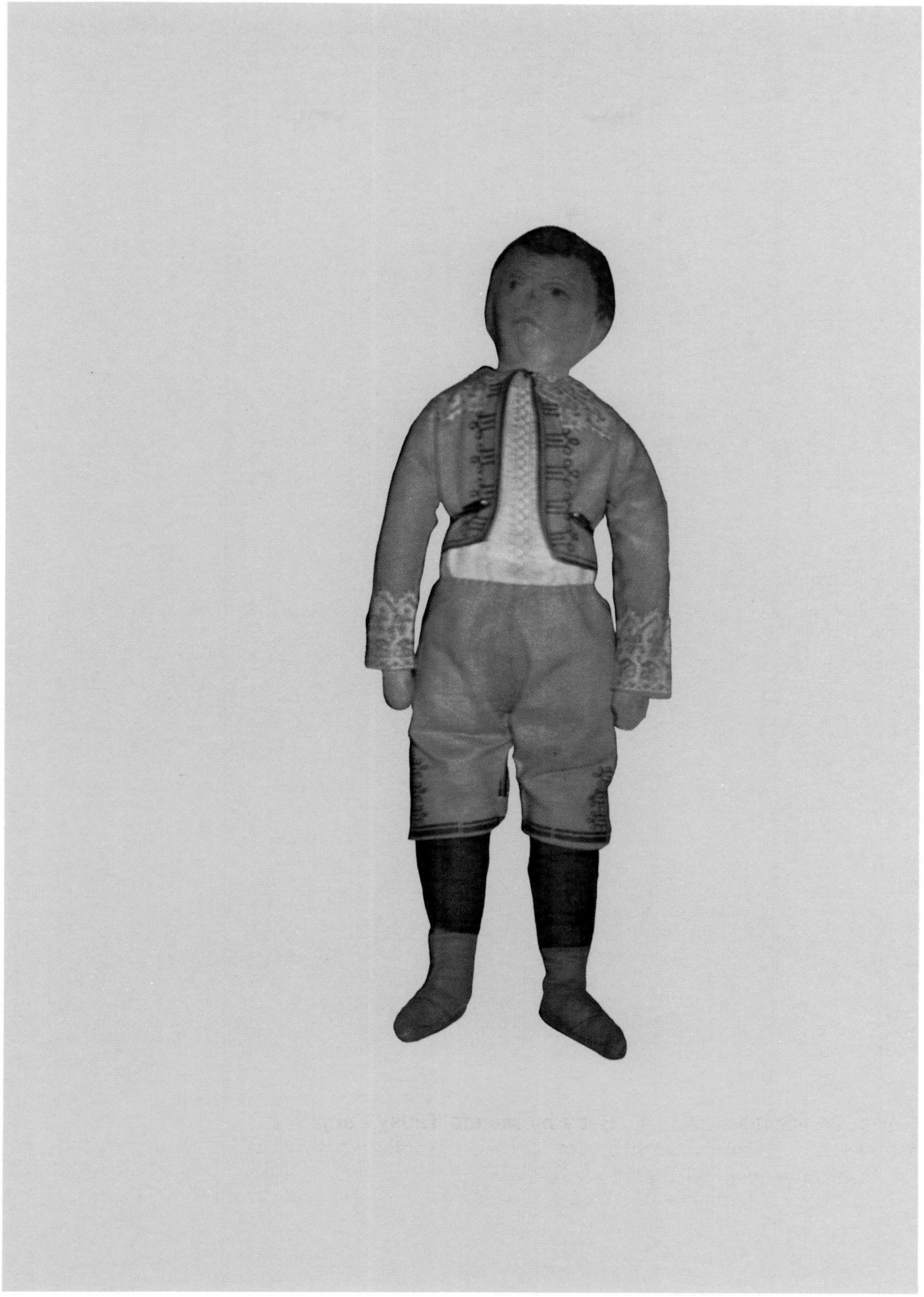

Collection of the late Barbara Graham

Type: 16'' Ida Gutsell Doll
Construction: *Body* - cut and sew pattern; stuffed with cotton; jointed at shoulders and hips; *Features* - lithographed, with some slight molding; *Clothes* - all original

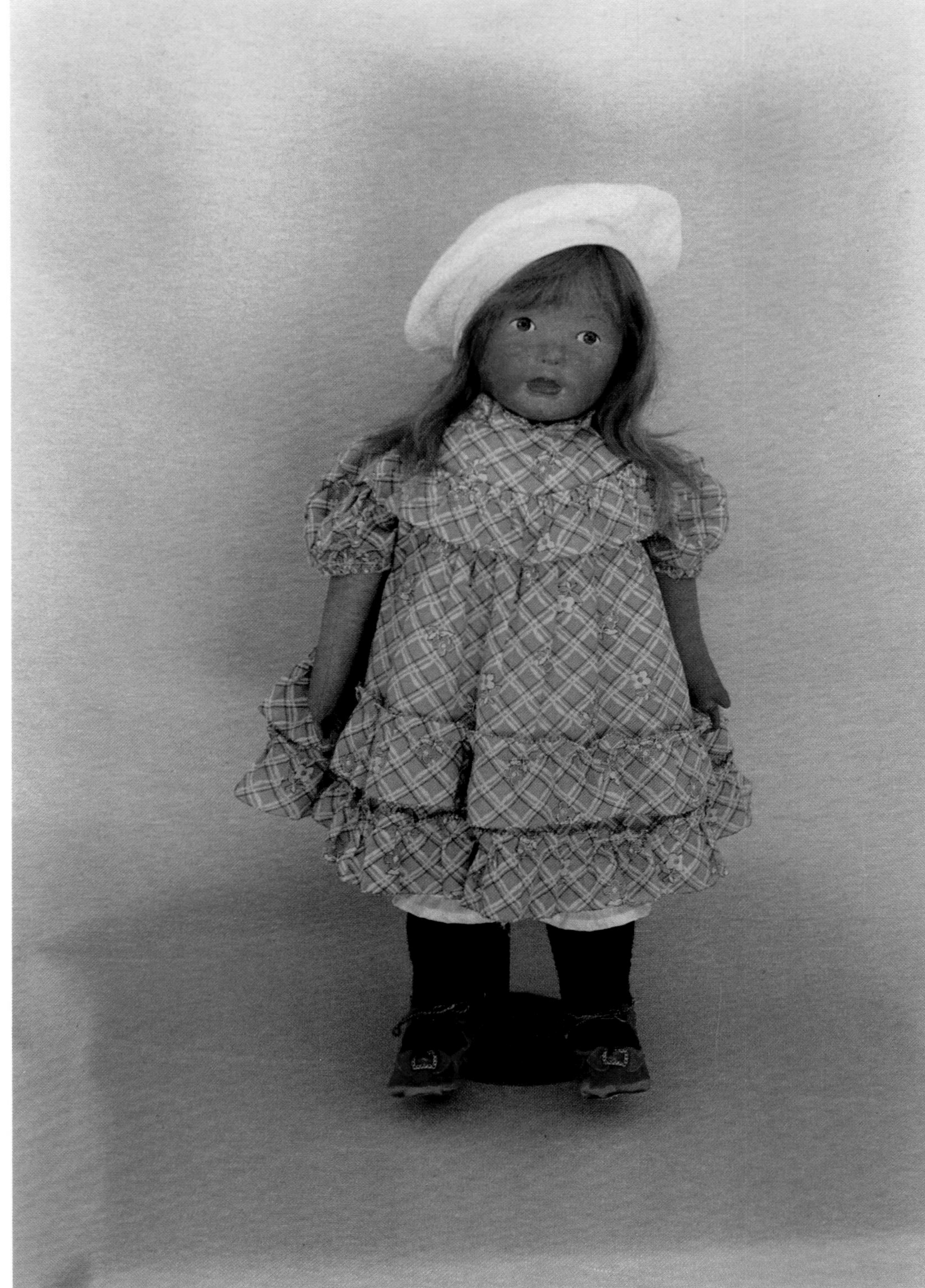

Collection of Margie Kimbro

Type: 19'' Kamkins

Construction: *Body* - heavy cotton jointed at the hips and shoulders; swivel head; *Hands* - fingers stitched with free standing thumbs; *Feet* - toes are stitched; *Features* - painted on a mask; original wig in a long style; mark found on back of head; this doll has a crier; *Clothes* - original

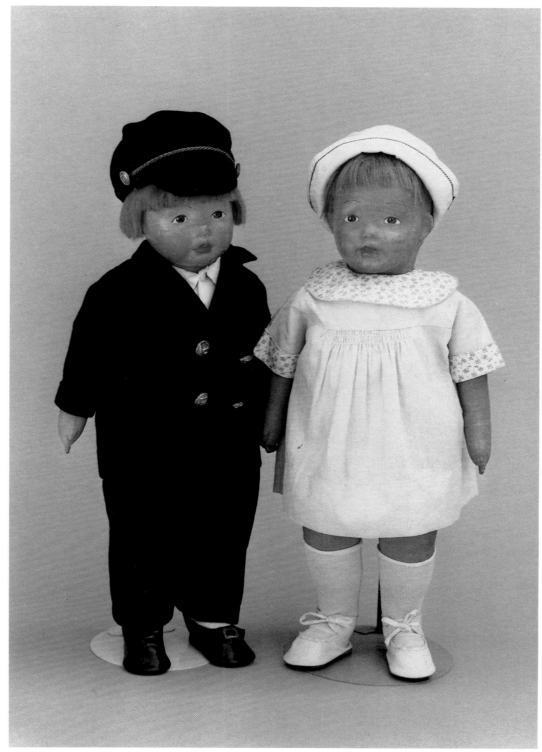

Collection of Mary Worrow

Type: 18" Kamkins Pair
Construction: *Body* - same as previous doll, minus the crier; *Features* - short mohair wig; mark on chest only; *Clothes* - original except for shoes

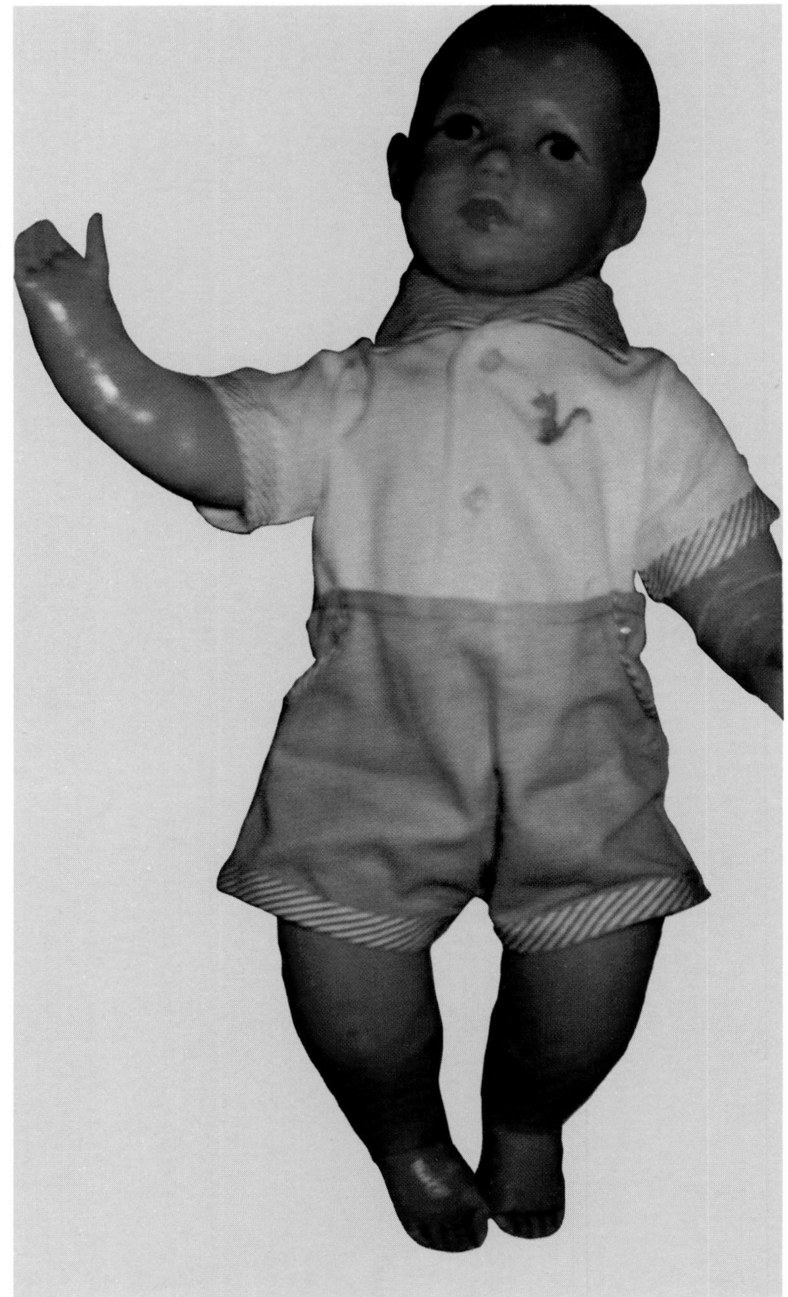

Collection of the late Barbara Graham

Type: 18'' Rare Kamkin Baby
Construction: *Body* - muslin; jointed at shoulders and hips; *Limbs* - painted with stitched fingers and toes; bent limb legs; *Features* - painted with painted hair; *Clothes* - old

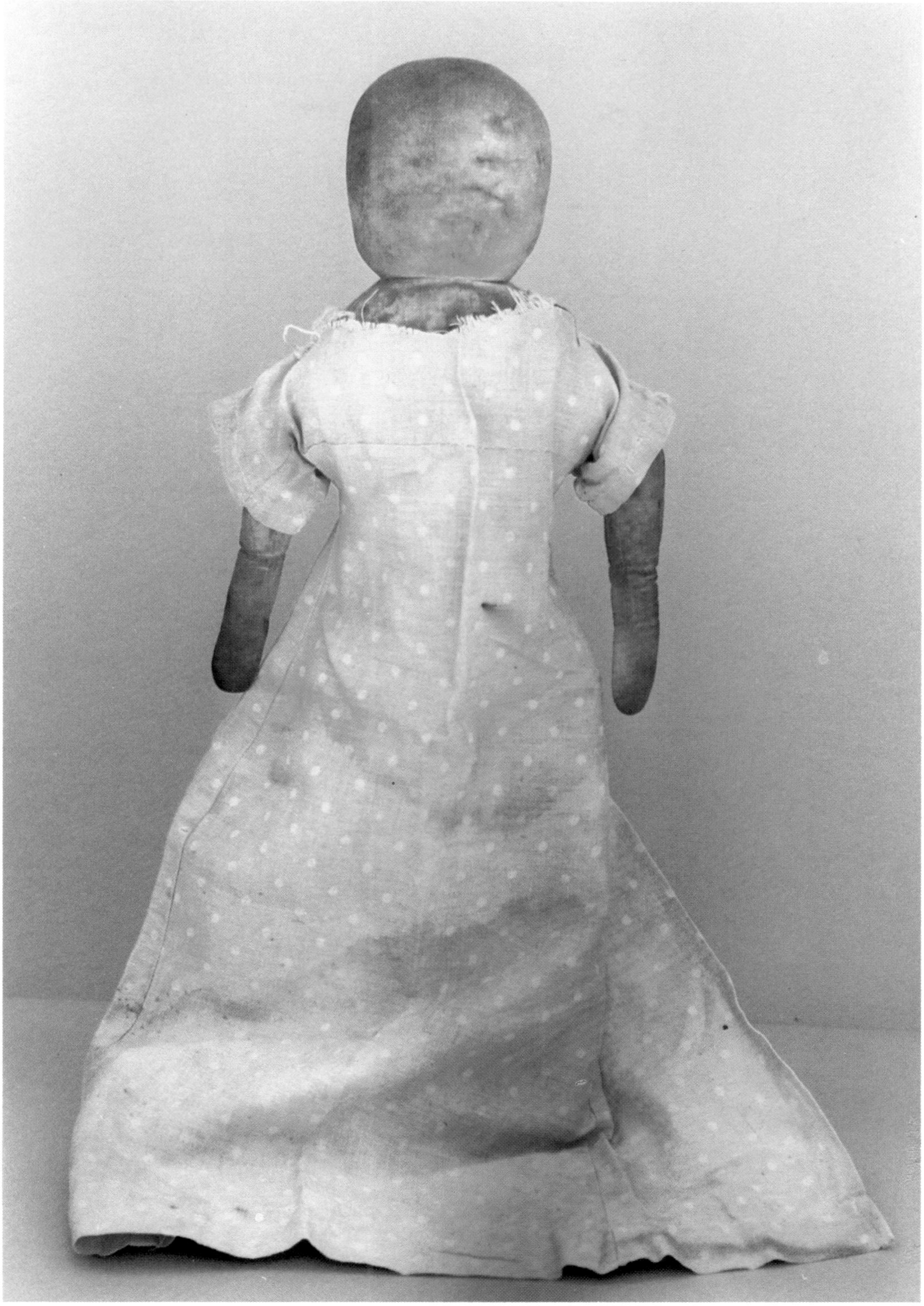

Courtesy of Pippen Hill Antiques

Type: 17'' Mother Congress Doll
Construction: *Body* - unbleached cotton stuffed with cotton; jointed at shoulders, hips and knees; *Hands* - stubs; *Features* - lithographed; round head; *Clothes* - old

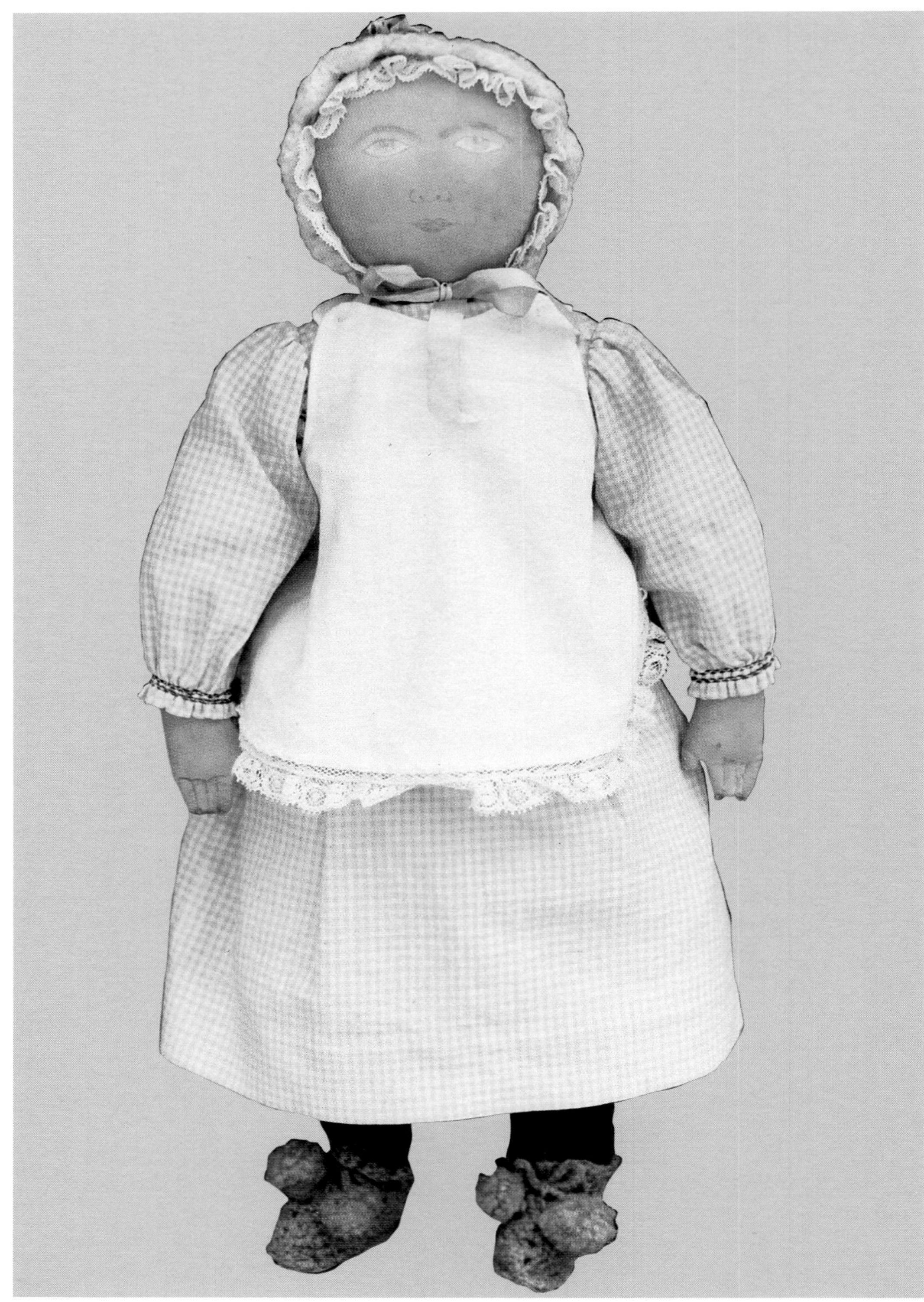
Author's Collection

Type: 16'' Moravian Rag (older version) (This doll dated early 1900s)
Construction: *Body* - cotton fabric jointed at hips, knees and shoulders; *Hands* - fingers are stitched with free-standing thumbs; *Feet* - stubs; *Features* - hand drawn; very softly painted; no hair (ruffled stitched around face); *Clothes* - original dress and pinafore

Collection of the late Barbara Graham

Type: 17" Pair of Older Moravian Dolls
Construction: *Body* - cotton stuffed with cotton; *Hands* - stitched fingers; *Features* - softly painted; painted hair; *Clothes* - all original

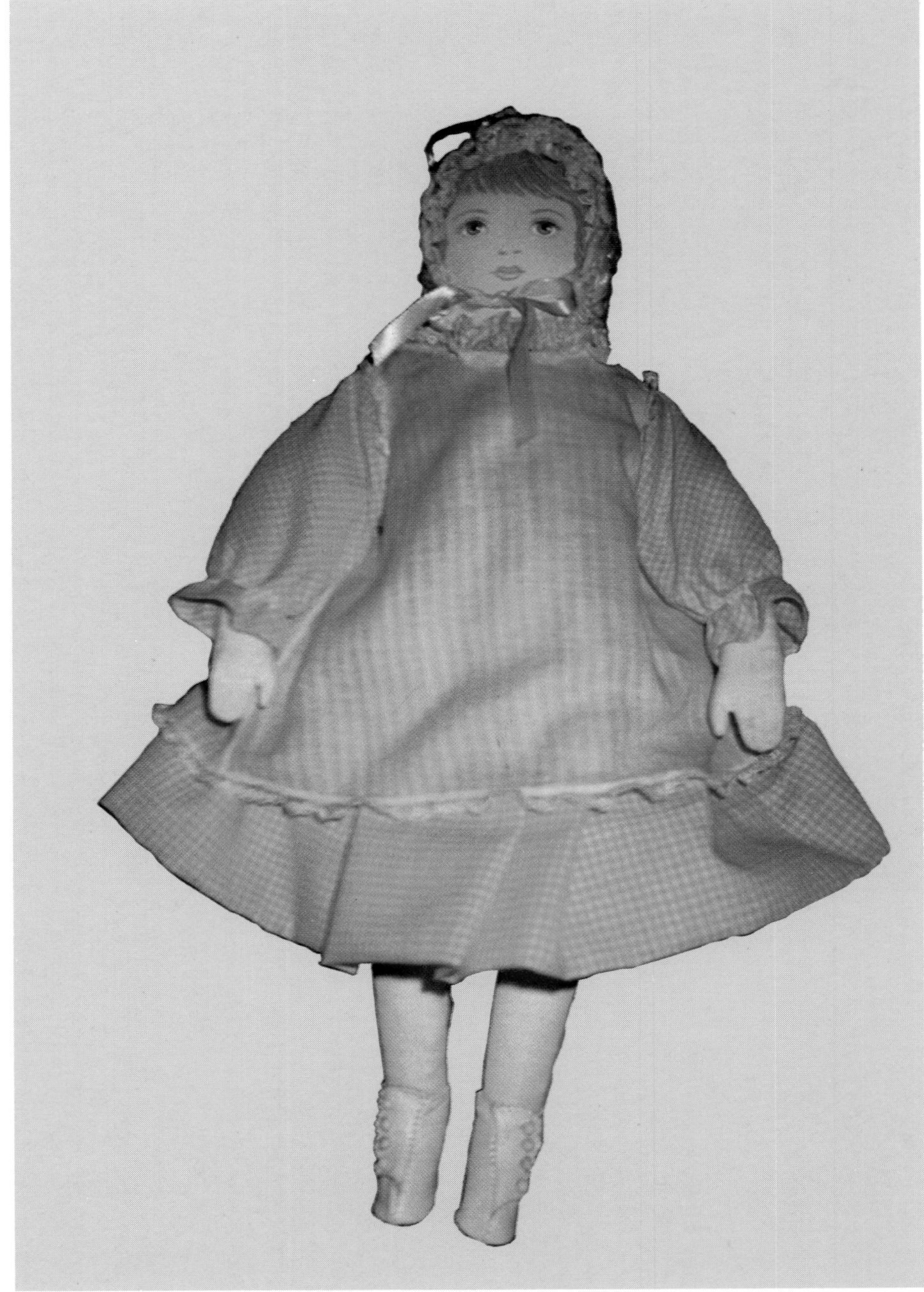

Collection of the late Barbara Graham

Type: 18" Later Moravian Doll
Construction: *Body* - cotton stuffed with cotton; *Hands* - stitched fingers; *Features* - brightly painted; painted hair; *Clothes* - original; *Note difference between old and newer version*

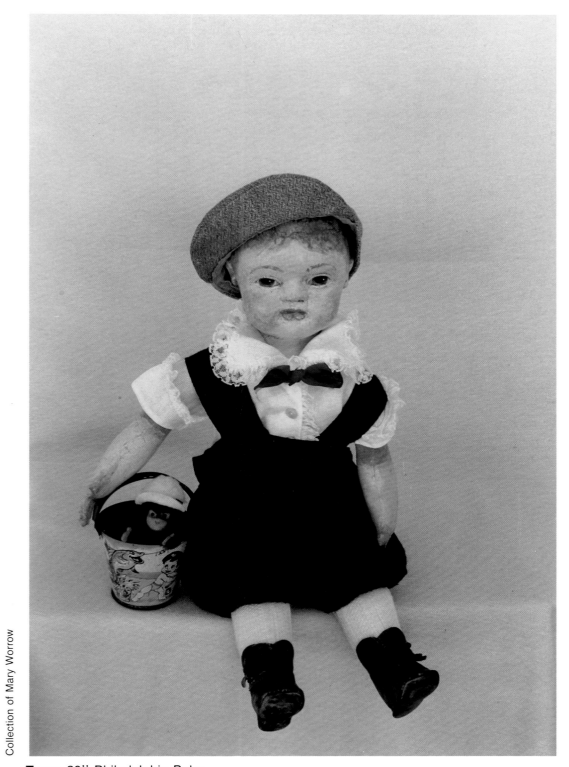

Collection of Mary Worrow

Type: 20" Philadelphia Baby

Construction: *Body* - stockingnette stuffed with cotton; jointed at hips, knees and shoulders; *Hands* - stitched fingers; painted almost to top of the arm; *Feet* - stitched toes; painted midway to top of leg; *Features* - molded and painted; ears are applied; these dolls have no mark; *Clothes* - old, not original

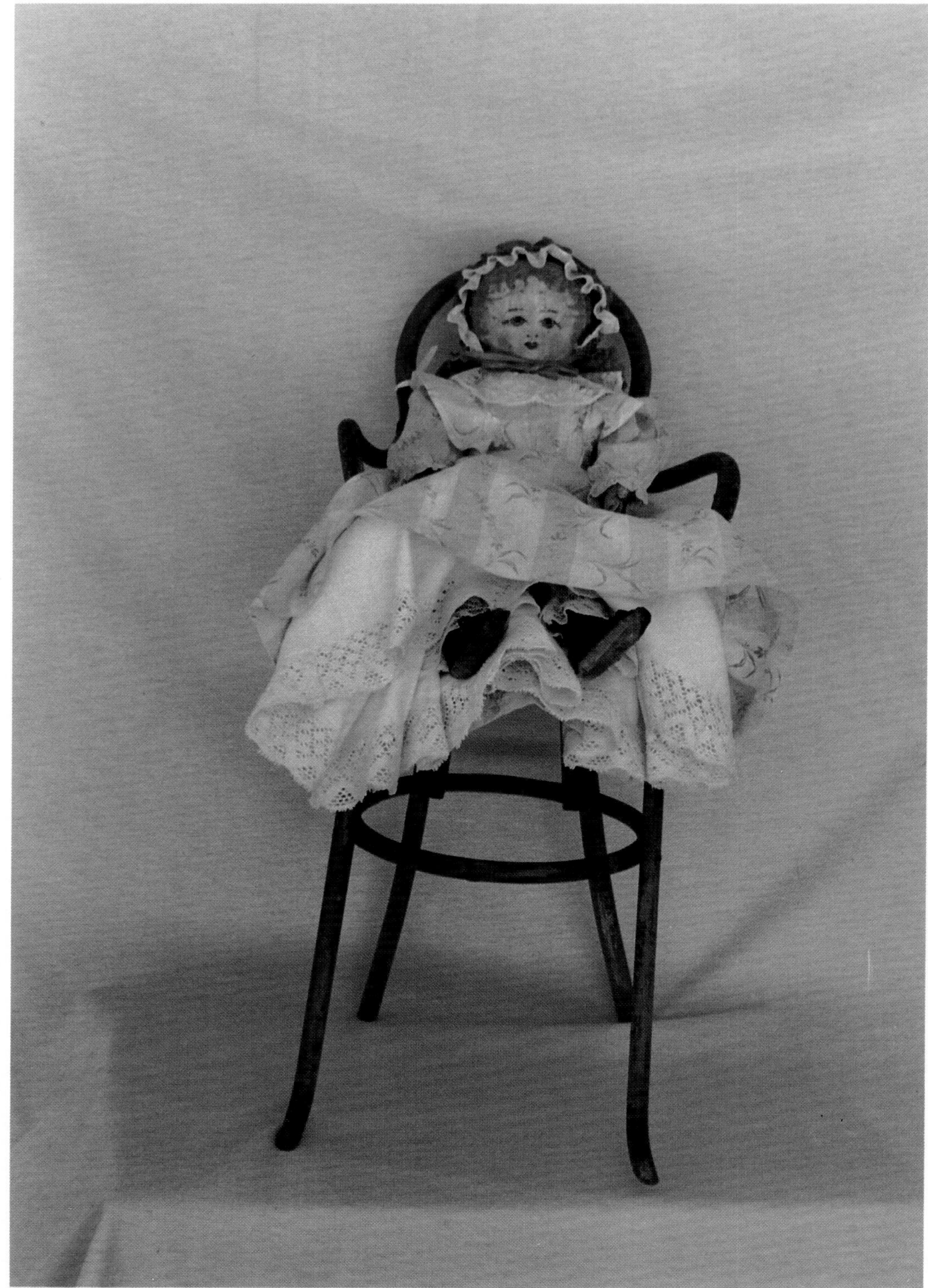

Author's Collection

Type: 17" Presbyterian Rag of Late 1800s
Construction: *Body* - unbleached cotton stuffed with cotton; jointed at shoulders; hips; *Hands* - stitched fingers; separate thumbs; *Feet* - stubs covered by long black stockings and handmade black leather shoes; *Features* - oil painted; head is flat sided, back and front; *Clothes* - original underclothes, socks and shoes; dress and bonnet are old replacements

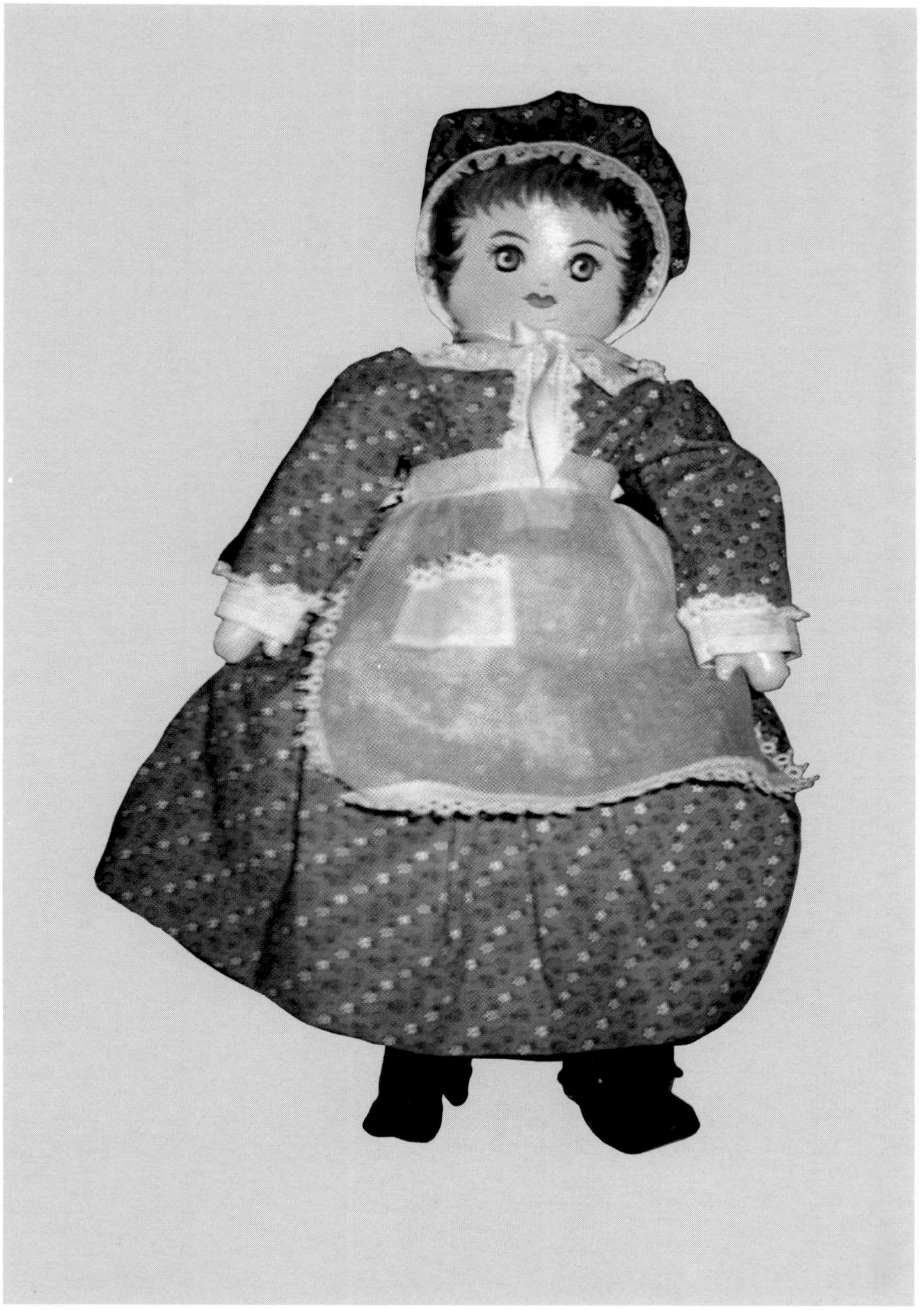

Collection of the late Barbara Graham

Type: 15" 1956 Presbyterian Rag Doll
Construction: *Body* - cotton stuffed with cotton; *Hands* - mitts; *Features* - heavily painted in oils; *Clothes* - original

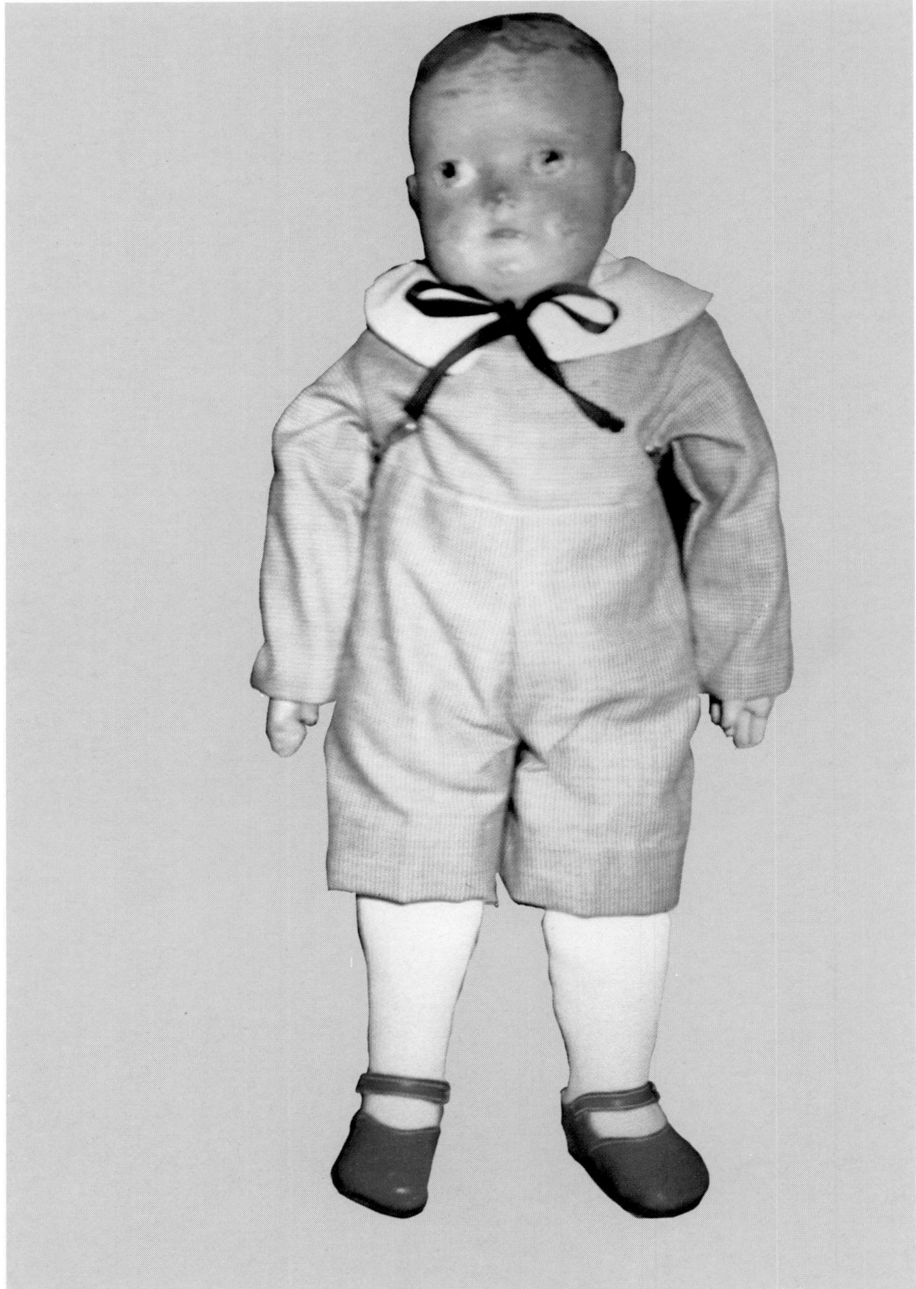

Collection of the late Barbara Graham

Type: 17'' Rollinson

Construction: *Body* - sateen jointed at knees, hips, elbows and shoulders; *Hands* - stitched fingers with separate thumbs; *Feet* - stitched toes; *Features* - molded stockingnette with many coats of paints; *Clothes* - old, not original

Author's Collection

Type: 20'' Possible Early Izannah Walker
Construction: *Body* - muslin stuffed with cotton; *Limbs* - applied ears; short hair style; painted; stitched fingers; *Features* - molded and oil painted; *Clothes* - old; *Note this doll has had much repair over the years but still retains her charm*

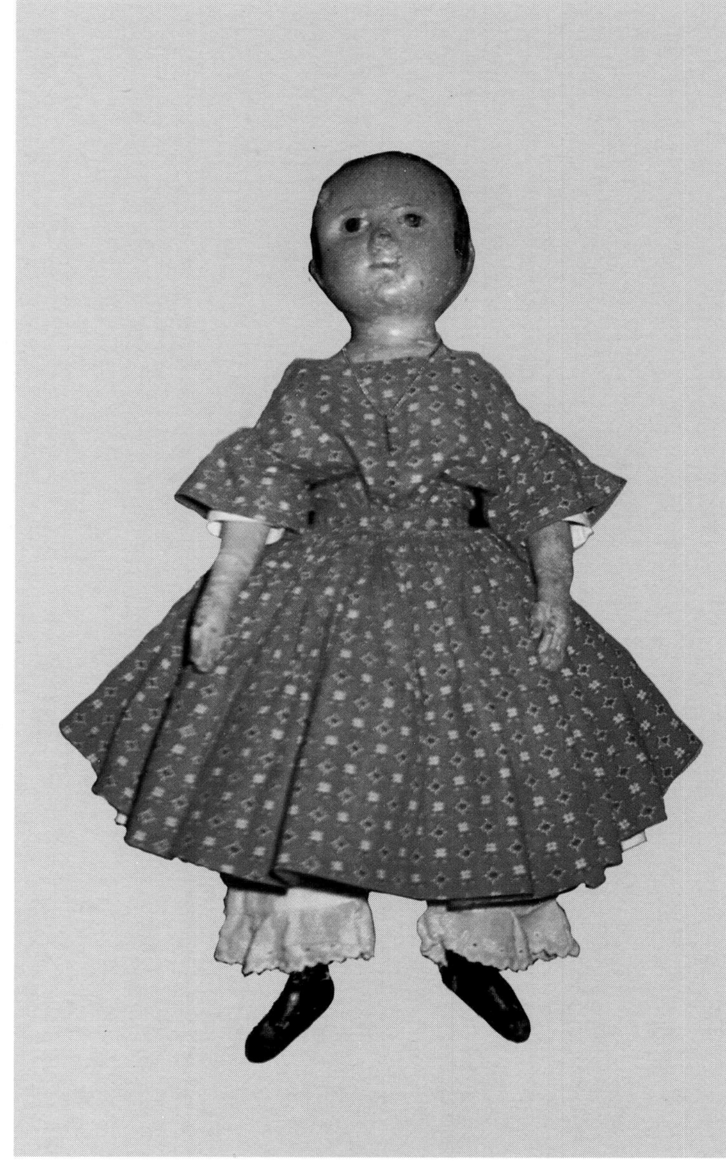
Collection of the late Barbara Graham

Type: 15'' Early Izannah Walker
Construction: *Body* - sateen stuffed with cotton; *Limbs* - painted; fingers are stitched; has painted boots; *Features* - molded and oil painted; applied ears; corkscrew side curls; *Clothes* - old

Chapter III

Raggedy Ann & Andy

Raggedy Ann is probably America's number one folk story. She came to be in 1914 when 12-year-old Marcella Gruelle (daughter of Johnny Gruelle) found an old faceless rag doll in the attic. It had belonged to her grandmother. Upon showing it to her father, she wished for it to have a face, so he immediately obliged and drew the features. These features have become timeless. She was then given her name from a poem by James Whitcomb Reilly, called Raggedy Man. From then on Raggedy Ann became Marcella's constant companion.

Marcella died when she was 14 years old. Out of intense grief and love, and in memory of his daughter, Johnny Gruelle began writing Raggedy stories. To promote his books, Raggedy Ann was placed along side them in a store window display. Customers were so taken with the doll that they wanted to purchase it, so orders began pouring in.

It is a misconception that Raggedy Andy was conceived at the same time as Ann, for it was a month later that Johnny Gruelle was contacted by a lady who had been a childhood friend of his mother's and had the brother to his mother's doll. A year later, after the family themselves had stopped making the doll and given the patent to Volland, did Andy join Ann. That is why the features and overall construction differ on the early Andy from the early Ann. At this time, Volland also began making the rest of the Raggedy characters found in the stories. They were: Uncle Clem, Beloved Belinde, Johnny Mouse, Percy Policeman, Cleety the Clown, Sunny Bunny and Brown Bear. Today these characters are not easily found. Many were discarded as no one knew what they were. Through the years, as different companies took over the patent rights, these characters were dropped except for Beloved Belinde. Knickerbocker did continue to produce her and introduced the Camel with the Wrinkled Knees. This was the only company to produce this character. It previously had only been available as a pattern put out around 1947 by McCall.

The pictures presented on the following pages are in order of the companies that produced the dolls from 1915 to the present.

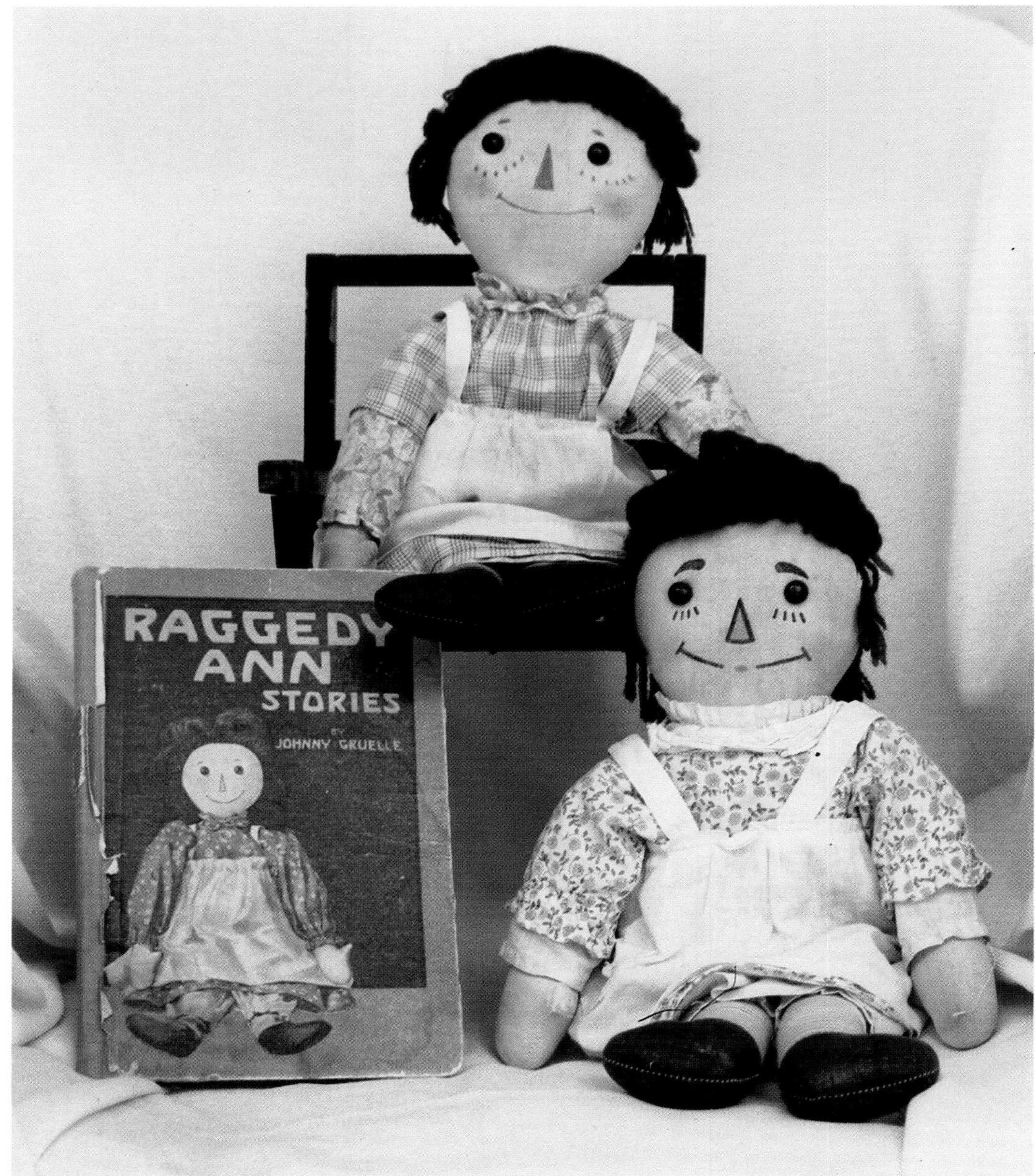

Collection of Sandra Thompson

Type: 15'' Early Gruelle Ann (upper left); 15'' Volland Ann (lower right)

Construction of Gruelle Ann: *Body* - unbleached cotton; mark on back of neck ''Patent 1915''; *Features* - hand painted with unbroken line for mouth; shoe button eyes; *Hair* - dark brown wool cruelle type yarn; *Clothes* - original; *Note - has wooden heart inside chest which is easily felt*

Construction of Volland Ann (circa 1918): *Body* - cotton; no mark; *Features* - printed, with broken line type mouth; shoe button eyes; *Hair* - dark brown wool yarn; *Clothes* - original; *Note - also has wooden heart inside chest*

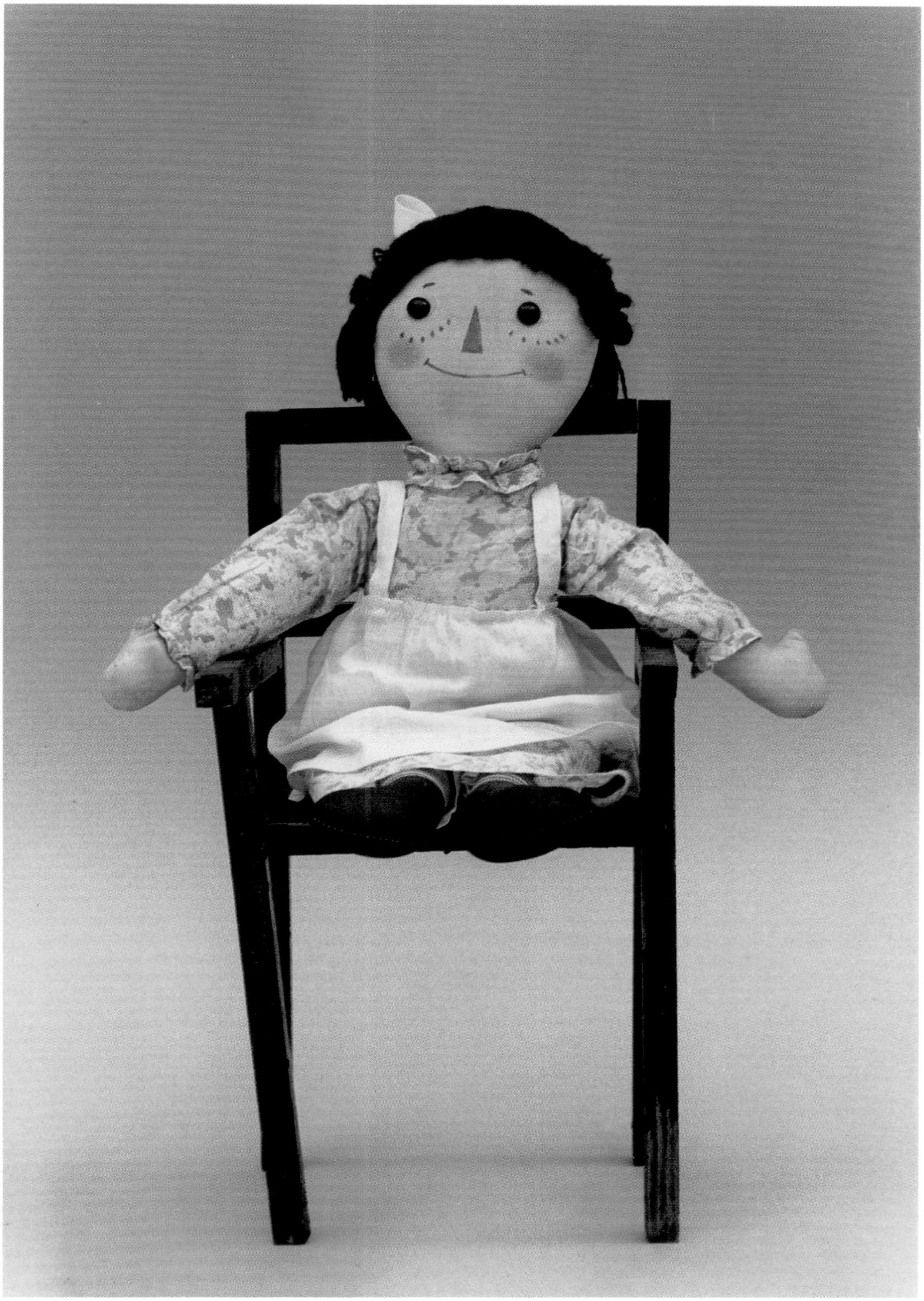

Author's Collection

Type: 15" Early Raggedy Ann
Construction: *Body* - unbleached cotton stuffed with cotton; has wooden heart inside chest area; has patent mark on back of neck so this is a Gruelle version; *Features* - hand painted; shoe button eyes; *Hair* - sparse brown wool yarn; *Clothes* - all original

Collection of Charlene Lucinian

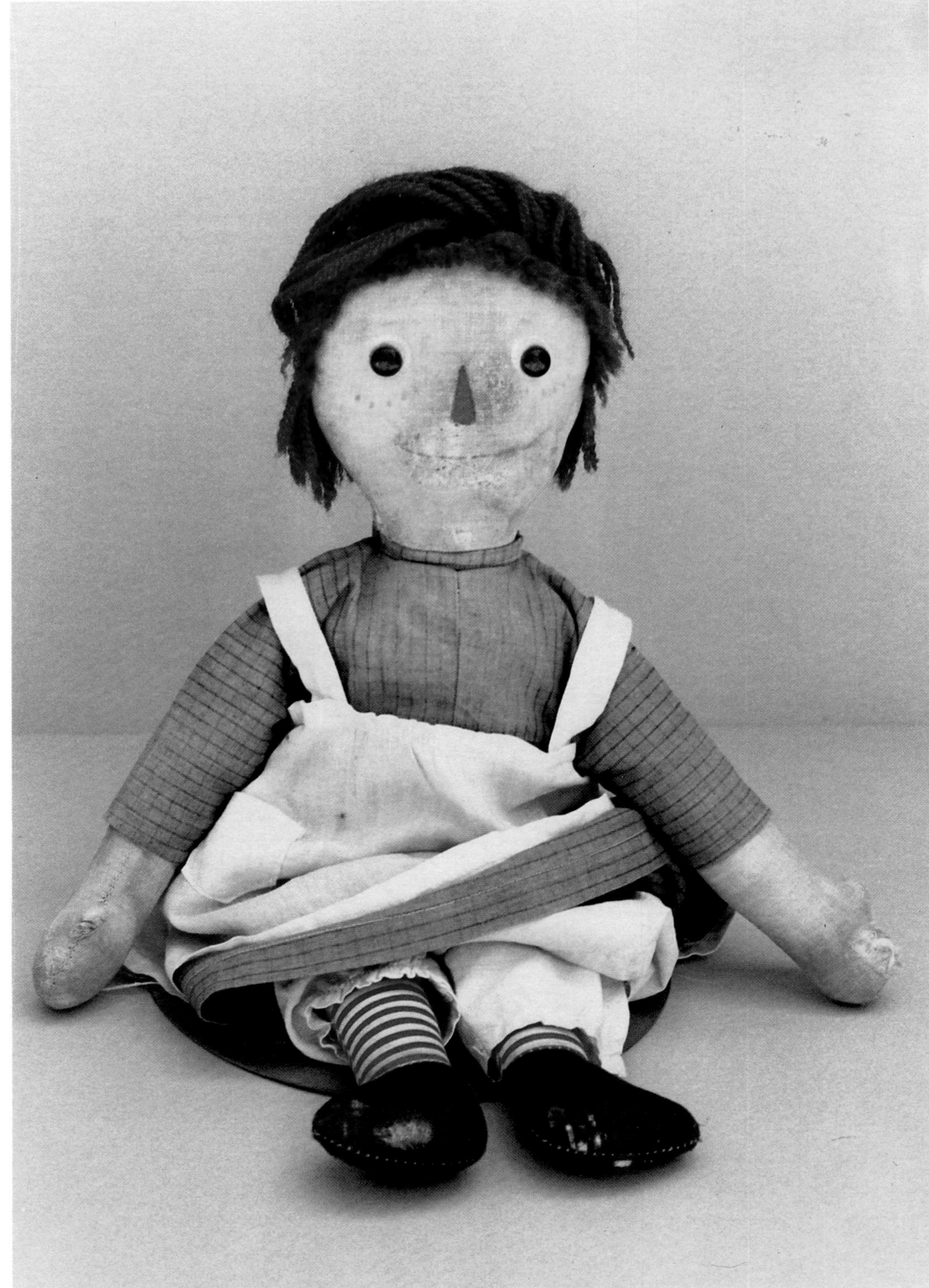

Type: 15" Early Raggedy Ann by Gruelle, 1915
Construction: *Body* - unbleached cotton stuffed with cotton; wooden heart inside chest area; *Features* - hand painted; shoe button eyes; *Hair* - brown wool yarn

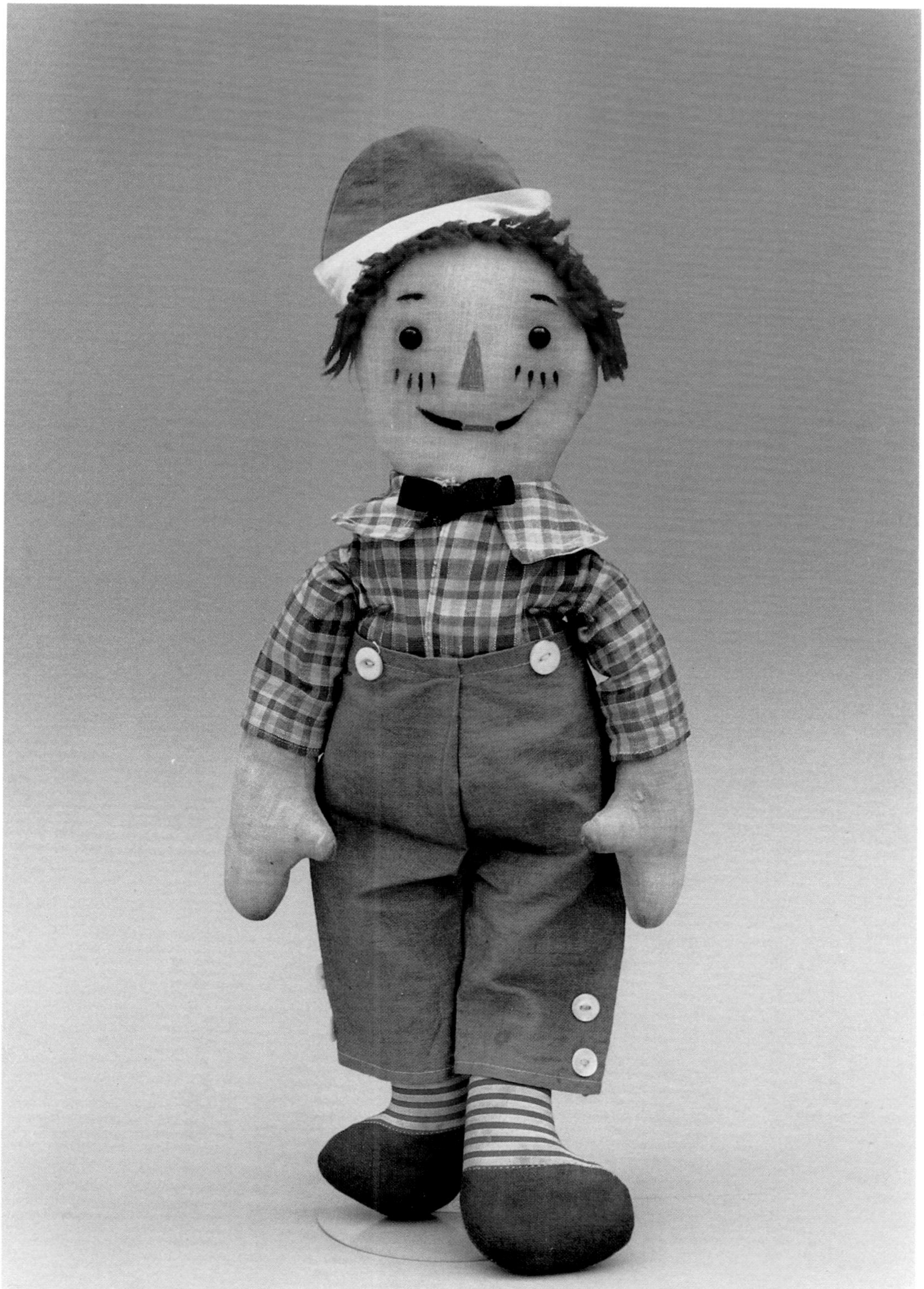

Author's Collection

Type: 15'' Volland Andy (first Andy) circa 1918

Construction: *Body* - cotton; no mark; *Features* - printed; shoe button eyes; *Hair* - sparse auburn colored wool yarn; *Clothes* - original, note pointed hat; *Note - Andy never had a wooden heart*

Author's Collection

Type: Pair 18'' 1920 Georgene Novelty Co. Raggedy Ann and Andy

Construction: *Body* - cotton; marked with tag found under left arm; tag reads, ''Johnny Gruelle's Own/Raggedy Ann & Andy Dolls/trade mark Reg. U.S. Patent Off./Copyright 1918-1920 By John B. Gruelle/Georgene Novelties Inc./New York City/Exclusive Licensed Manufacturers/Made in U.S.'' *Note - the last date on the tag is said to be the date of issue; Features* - printed with outlined nose; large flat shoe button eyes; *Hair* - auburn wool yarn; *Clothes* - original

Author's Collection

Type: Pair 18" Raggedy Ann & Andy by Mollye Goldman (circa 1920s)
Construction: *Body* - cotton; mark found on chest with printed heart which reads "Produced by Mollye's Doll Outfitters"; *Features* - printed with black outline around nose; *Hair* - light auburn wool yarn; *Clothes* - original, note socks have blue lines; shoes are blue

Collection of the late Barbara Graham

Type: 12" Awake-Asleep Raggedy Ann by Georgene Novelty Co. (circa 1920)
Construction: *Features* - printed on both sides of the head; a strip of bright auburn yarn is sewn going from one side of the head to the other; the eyes are metal buttons; *Clothes* - original

Collection of Sandra Thompson

Type: Pair 18'' 1947 Georgene Novelty Raggedy Ann & Andy
Construction: *Body* - cotton; marked with tag under left arm; last date being 1947; *Features* - printed; nose not lined; large flat metal eyes; *Hair* - light auburn; *Clothes* - original; *Note - dresses on the Georgene Raggedy Ann came in many different prints, as did the shirts on the Raggedy Andy.*

Collection of Carol Osbourn

Type: 15'' Raggedy Ann By Georgene Novelty Co.
Construction: *Body* - same as previously pictured Georgene's; this one still has her original tag

Author's Collection

Type: 18'' 1926 Georgene Novelty Beloved Belindy

Construction: *Body* - milk chocolate colored cotton; *Mark* - stamped on back of head, reads ''Johnny Gruelle's Own/Beloved Belindy/Trade mark Reg. U.S. Patent Office/Copyright 1926 by Johnny Gruelle/Georgene Novelties Inc. N.Y.C./Exclusive licensed Manufacturers; *Features* - painted; nose outlined; eyes are large white buttons; *Clothes* - original; has red shoes; doll is made having a large stomach

Collection of the late Barbara Graham

Type: 17'' Raggedy Ann Character, Uncle Clem (by Volland)
Construction: *Body* - cotton stuffed with cotton; *Features* - embroidered with yarn hair; large nose; *Clothes* - original; *Note - this is a hard to find doll.*

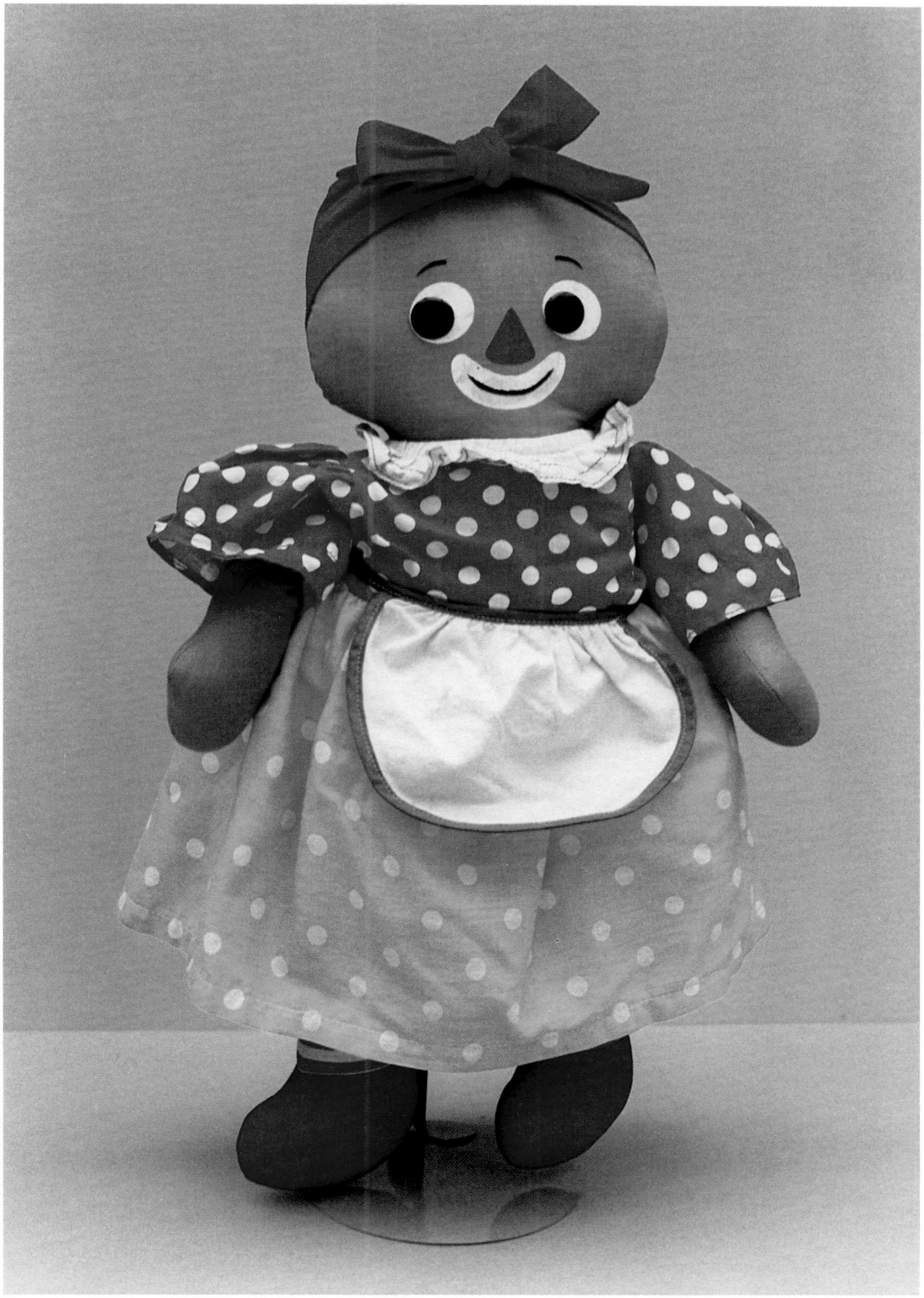

Collection of the late Barbara Graham

Type: 15'' Knickerbocker Beloved Belindy
Construction: *Body* - coffee-colored cotton material; *Features* - painted with large plastic eyes; mark is a tag sewn on side of doll; *Clothes* - original, missing apron

Author's Collection

Type: Camel With the Wrinkled Knees
Construction: *Body* - made from 1947 pattern; was not produced by any company at this time

Author's Collection

Type: Pair of 15" Raggedy Ann & Andy Copies
Construction: *Body* - cotton; heads are oilcloth; no mark, but these dolls are attributed to the American Novelty Manufacturing Co.; they date from 1940s to late 1950s and were called Buddy Huggable Nursery Pet; *Features* - painted; *Hair* - bright auburn wool yarn; *Clothes* - original, sewn directly onto the body; note the oddly printed legs

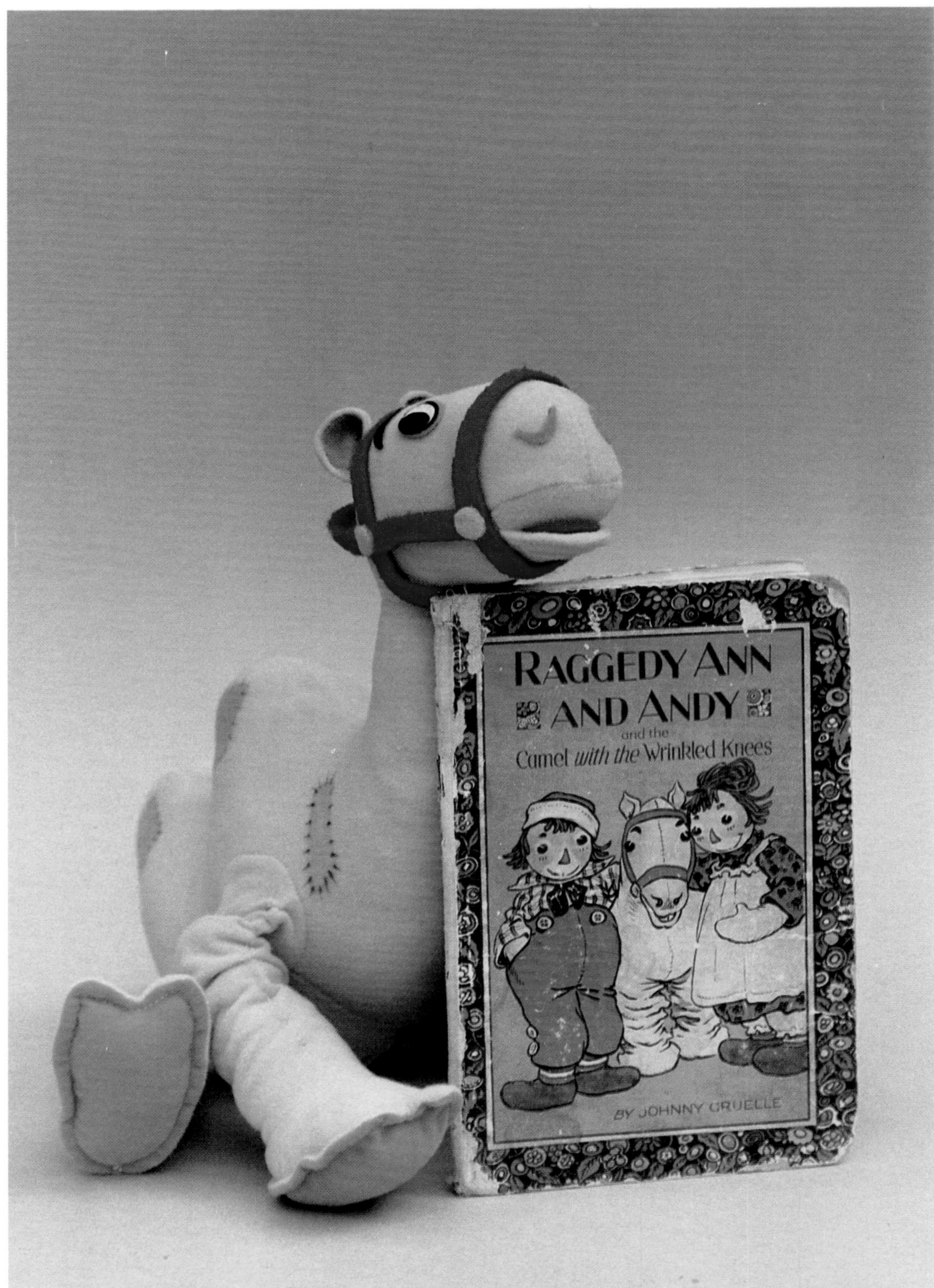

Collection of Sandy Thompson

Type: Knickerbocker Camel with the Wrinkled Knees (circa 1965)
Construction: *Body* - flannel type material with felt accents; *Features* - felt; *Note - this was the only company that made this character*

Collection of the late Barbara Graham

Type: 6'' Long Knickerbocker Raggedy Arthur
Construction: *Body* - synthetic fabric; yarn hair

Collection of Margie Kimbro

Type: 19" Homemade Ann (circa 1930s)
Construction: *Body* - cotton stuffed with cotton; *Features* - embroidered with outlined nose (aids in dating); button eyes; *Hair* - light rust-colored yarn; *Clothes* - original to the doll; *Note - this is a well done example*

Author's Collection

Type: 18" 1930s Handpainted Raggedies
Construction: *Body* - unbleached cotton stuffed with cotton; *Features* - painted; *Hair* - bright red wool yarn; *Clothes* - all original

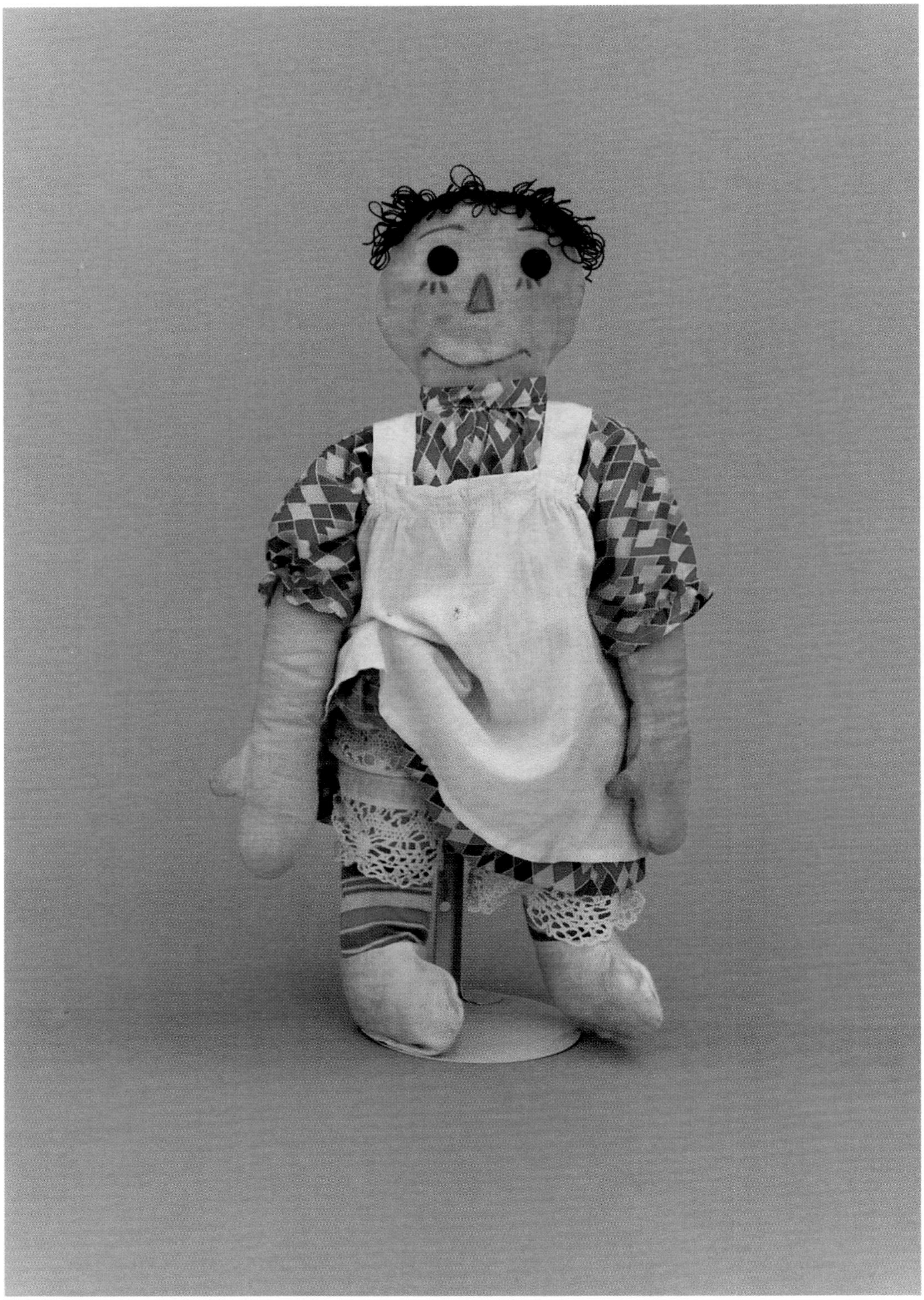

Collection of Mary Worrow

Type: 18" Homemade Raggedy Ann (circa 1920s)
Construction: *Body* - unbleached cotton stuffed with cotton; note the large hands; *Features* - painted; nose outlined; large button eyes; *Hair* - dark auburn string; *Clothes* - original to the doll; this doll has a great deal of charm

Collection of Mary Worrow

Type: 18" Homemade Raggedies (circa 1930s)
Construction: *Body* - unbleached cotton stuffed with cotton; *Features* - embroidered with a lot of detail; nose outlined; *Hair* - bright auburn embroidery floss styled in tiny hard curls; *Clothes* - all original; *Note - this is a magnificently done pair!*

Chapter IV

Rag Dolls Made From 1930s to 1950s

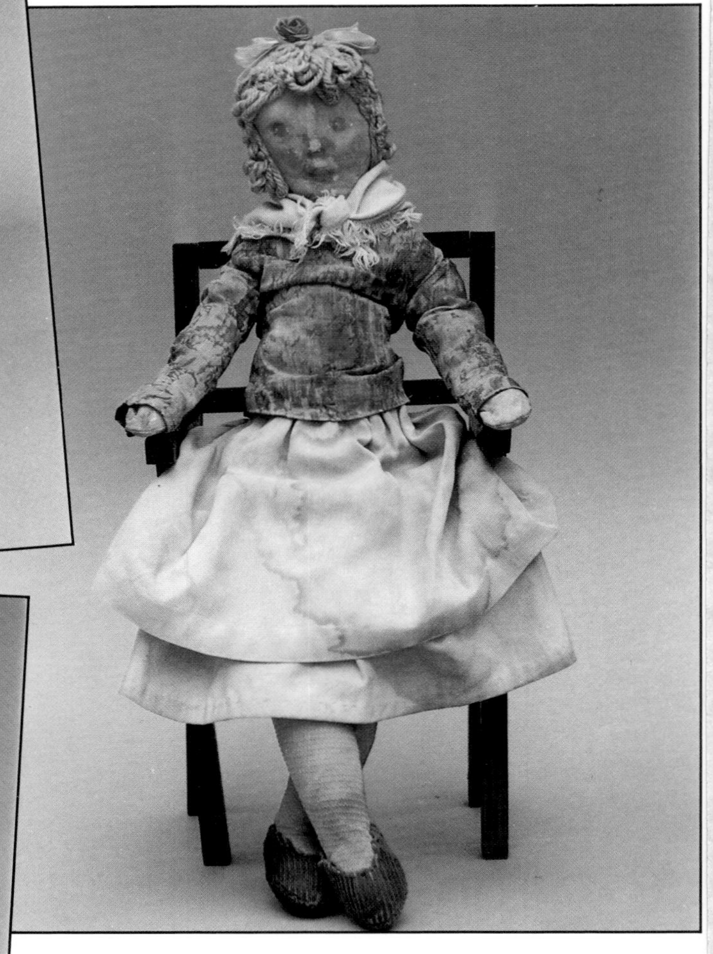

The years from 1930 through 1950 were very successful years for the rag doll. Many American companies were now manufacturing rag dolls.

The following pages will only include a few of the homemade and unknown types. There is already a book on the market that covers the manufactured rag dolls of this period in detail.

This particular style of rag doll has not been my forte. My knowledge lies primarily with the older rags. I have included these for the collector to get a general idea of the difference between the turn-of-the-century types and these types.

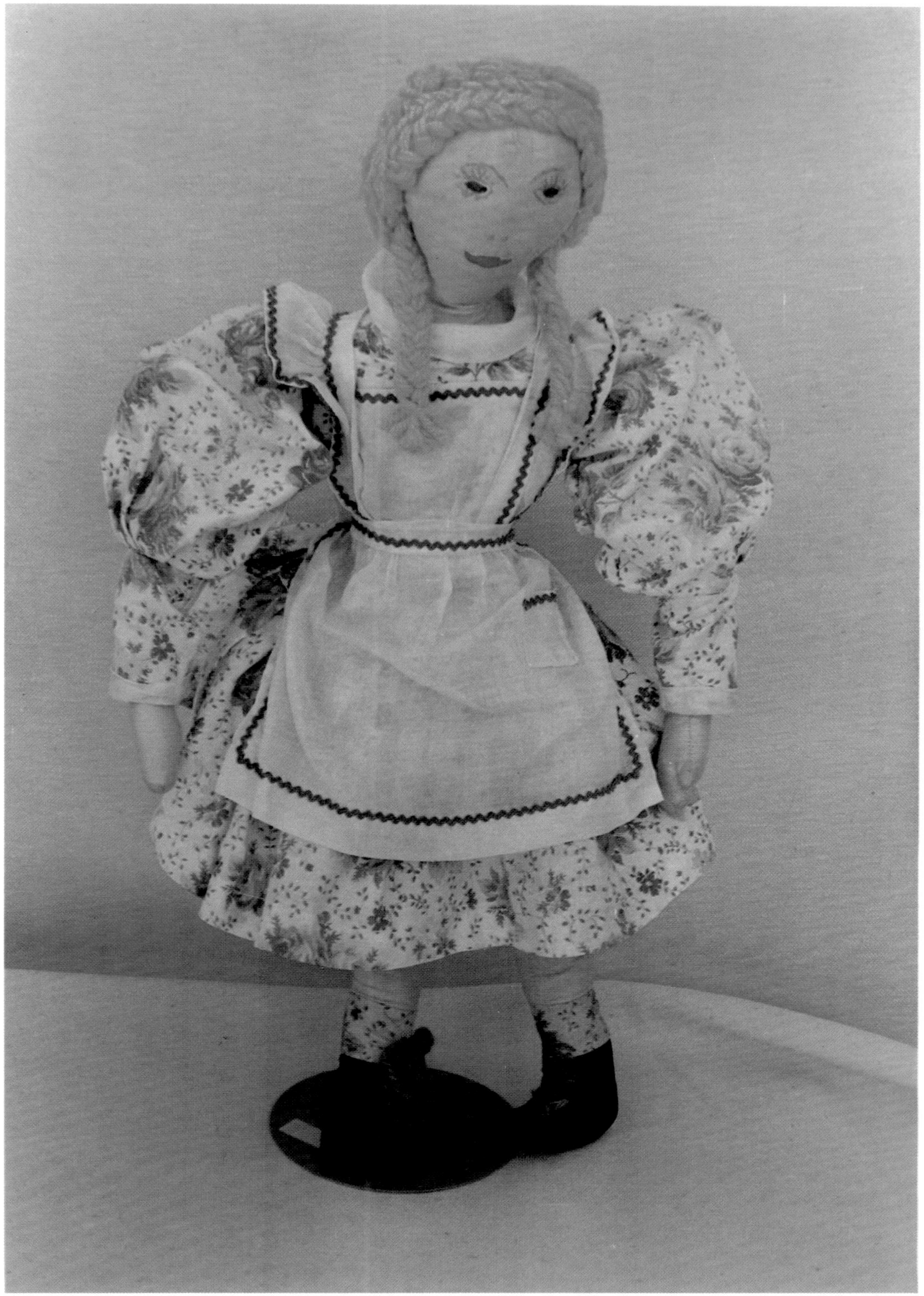

Author's Collection

Type: 18" Homemade (circa Late 20s, Early 30s Rag)
Construction: *Body* - polished cotton; jointed at hips and shoulders; *Features* - embroidered; *Hair* - wool yarn; *Clothes* - original flour sack-type material; organdy apron

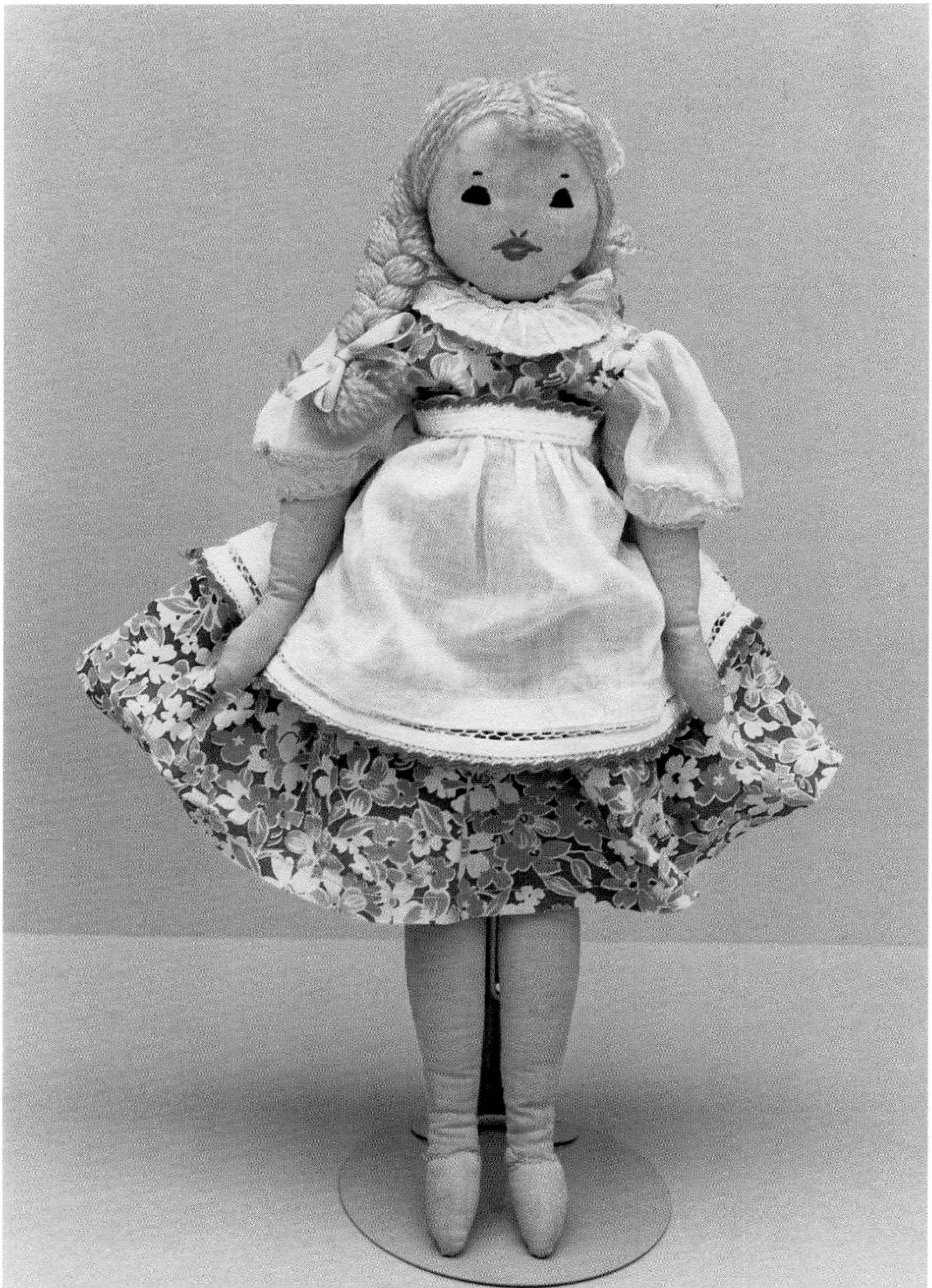

Author's Collection

Type: Homemade Rag Doll (circa 1936)
Construction: *Body* - polished cotton stuffed with cotton; jointed at shoulders and hips; *Features* - stitched; *Hair* - wool yarn; *Clothes* - all original; *Note - this doll was a gift from the original owner*

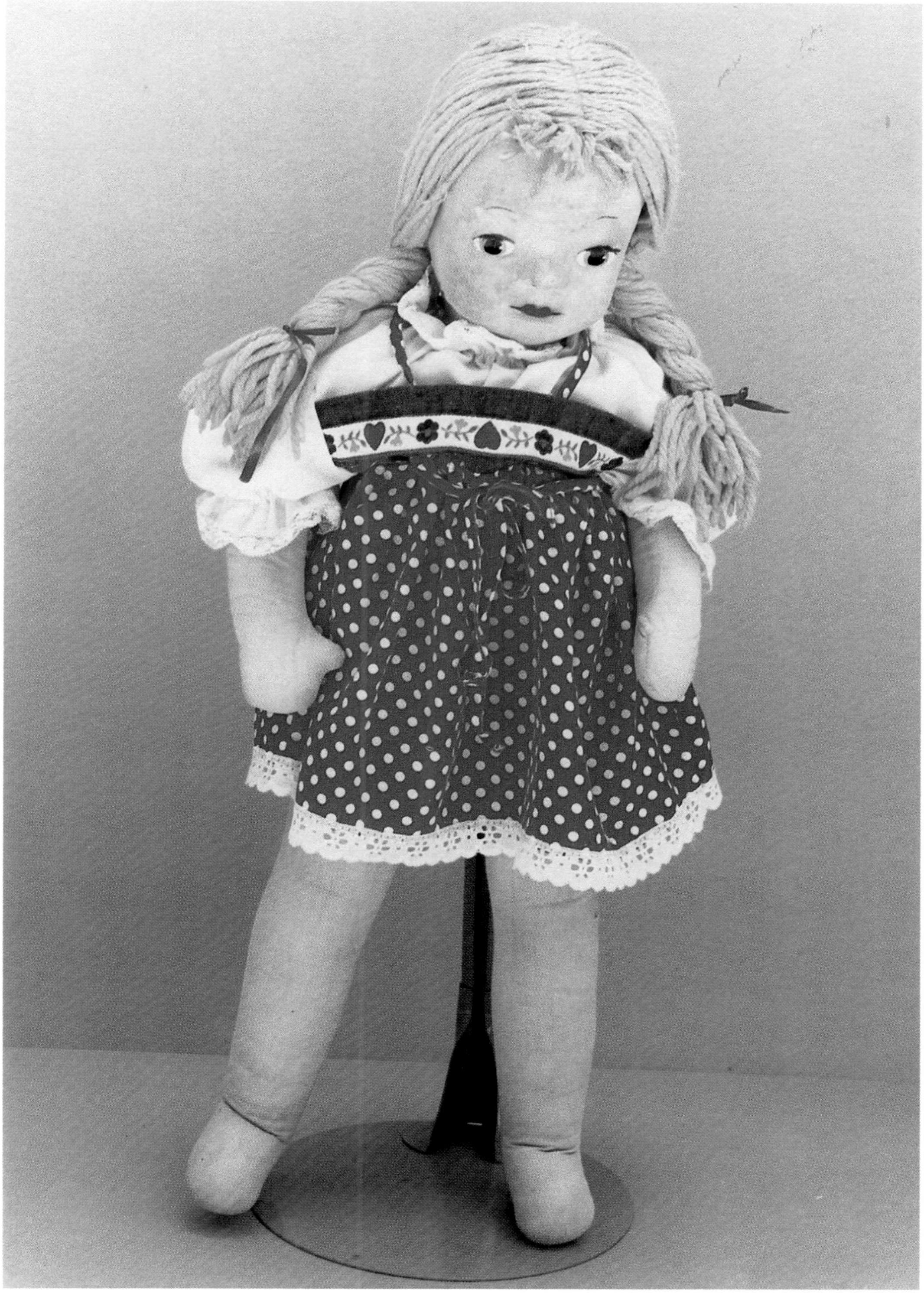

Collection of Charlene Lucinian

Type: 24" Mask Face Rag Doll (circa 1940)
Construction: *Body* - cotton stuffed with cotton; swivel head; *Features* - painted with hair eyelashes; *Hair* - rug yarn; *Clothes* - old, not original

Author's Collection

Type: Homemade Rag Boy (circa 1930s-1940s)
Construction: *Body* - cotton stuffed with cotton; jointed at hips and shoulders; has little boots as part of leg; *Features* - stitched; *Hair* - wool yarn; *Clothes* - old

Author's Collection

Type: Black Rag Doll (circa late 1940s, early 1950s)
Construction: *Body* - black stocking stuffed with foam rubber; applied ears; *Features* - stitched and appliqued with two upper teeth; *Hair* - black yarn

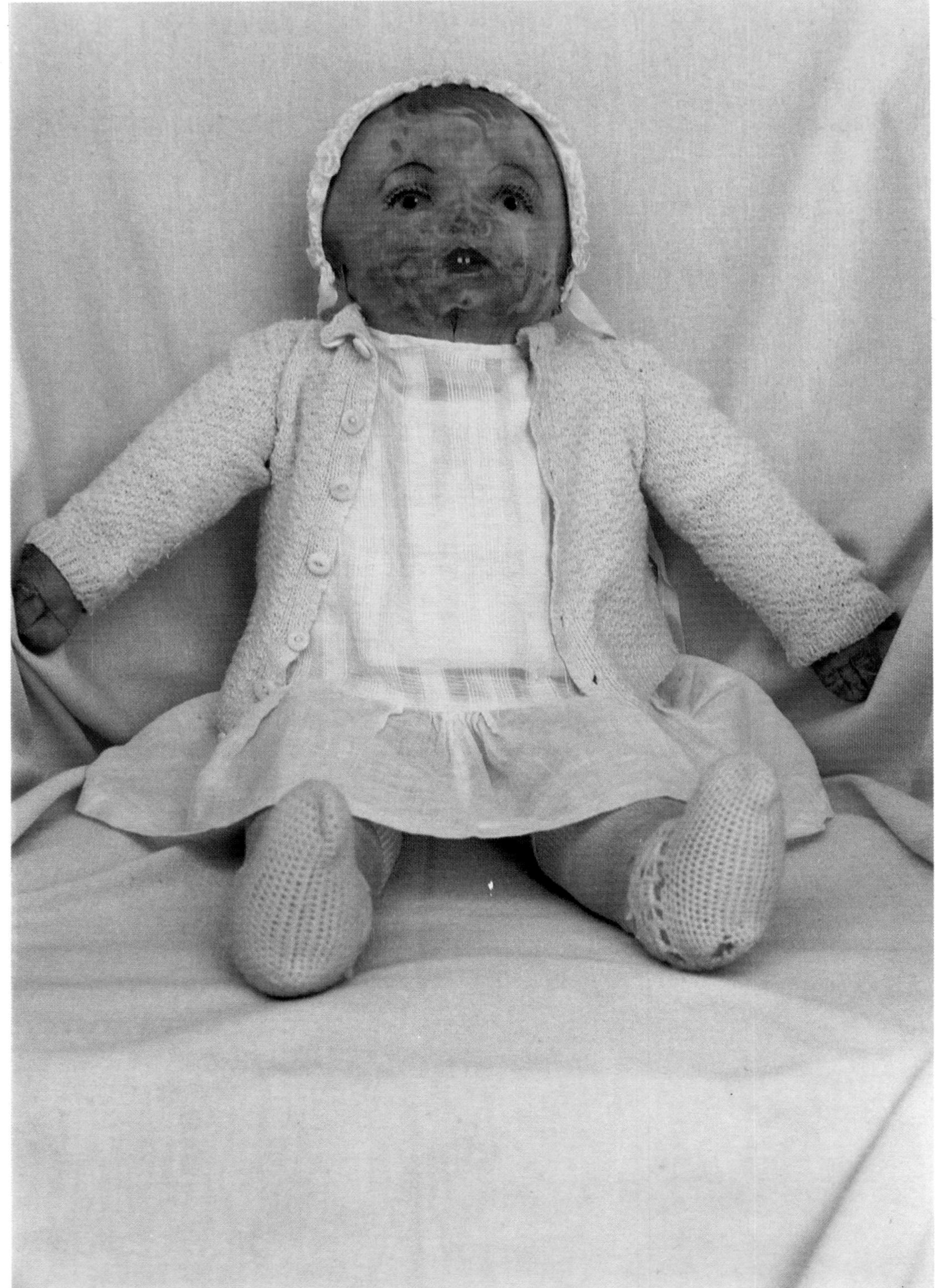

Collection of Margie Kimbro

Type: 22" Mask Face Rag (circa 1930s)
Construction: *Body* - muslin stuffed with straw; jointed and hips and shoulders; *Features* - painted on a mask which is secured to the head by means of a cord; *Clothes* - old, not original

Author's Collection

Type: 16" Homemade Rag (circa 1930s)
Construction: *Body* - cotton stuffed with cotton; jointed at shoulders and hips; *Features* - painted; head rounded with several seams; *Hair* - wool yarn; *Clothes* - old, not original

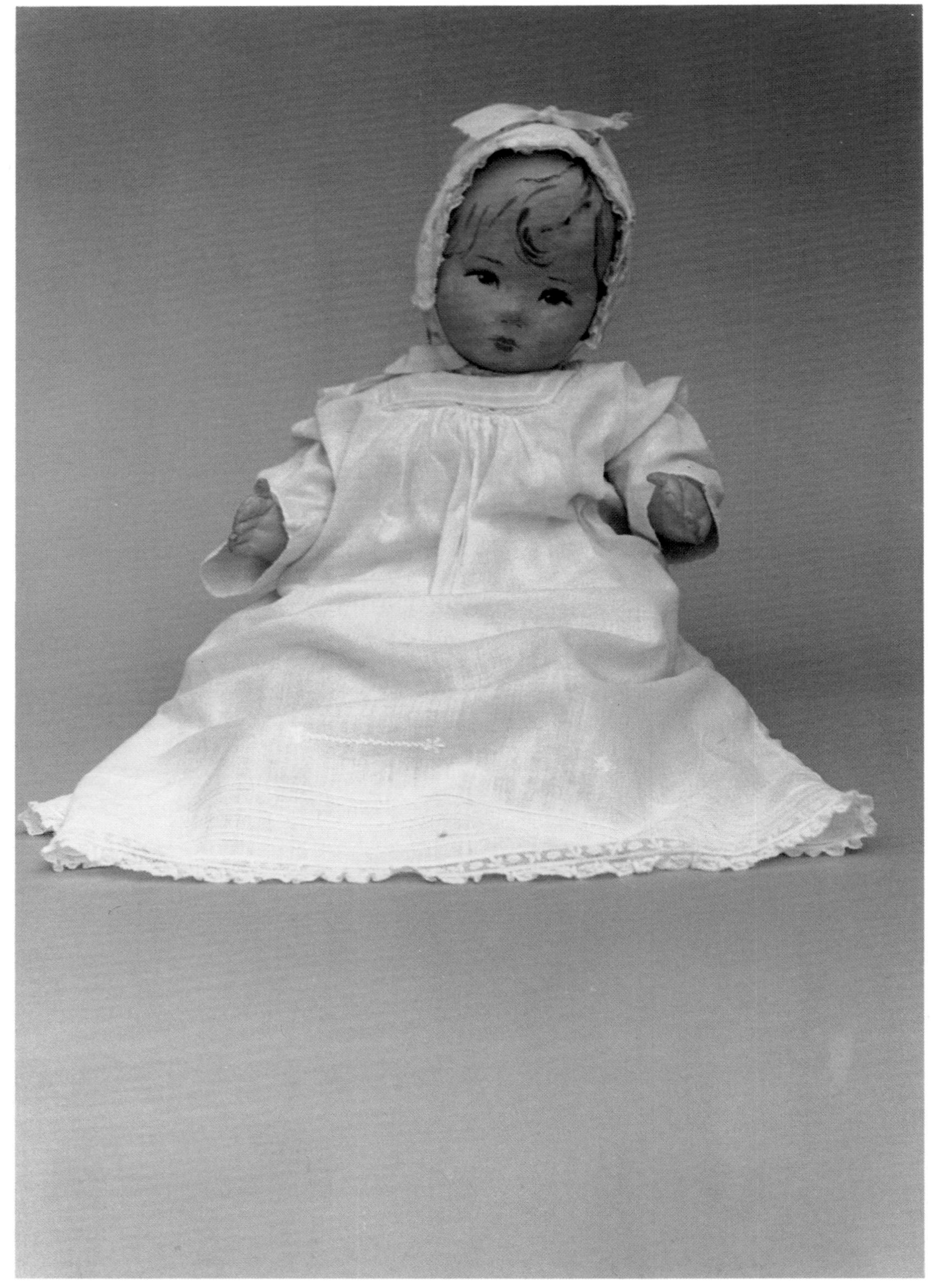

Author's Collection

Type: 22'' Manufactured Mask Face Rag Baby (circa late 1920s, early 1930s)

Construction: *Body* - pink cotton; hard stuffed with cotton; disc jointed at hips and shoulders; *Features* - painted on a mask; applied to head by stitching; *Head* - round and swivel with a layer of plaster over the stuffing, giving it some weight; *Clothes* - old, not original

Author's Collection

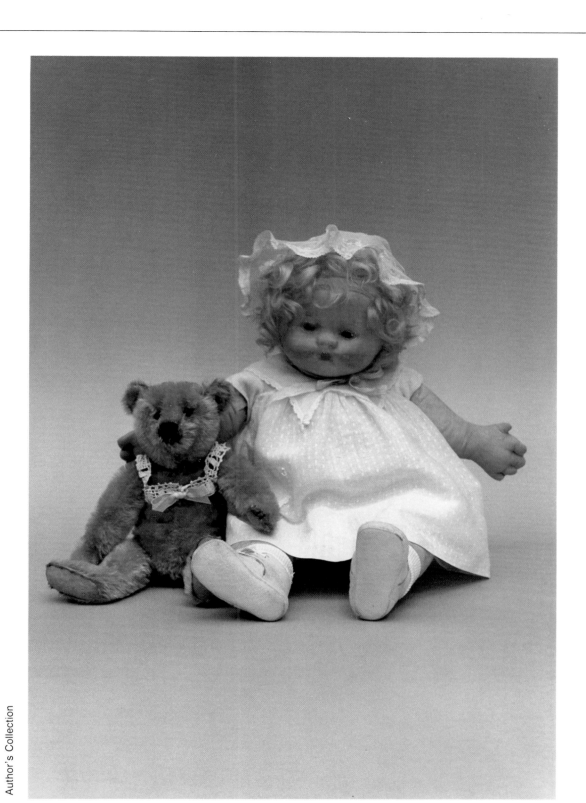

Type: 23'' Manufactured Mask Face Baby (circa 1930s, 1940s)
Construction: *Body* - polished cotton stuffed with cotton; jointed at hips and shoulders; *Features* - painted on a mask with real hair lashes (this is a feature of Georgene Novelty Co. and Madame Alexander); *Head* - swivel with mohair wig; *Clothes* - old, not original

Author's Collection

Type: 15" Manufactured Rag (circa late 1930s, early 1940s)

Construction: *Body* - hard stuffed cotton; jointed at hips and shoulders; *Features* - embroidered; *Hair* - wool yarn; *Clothes* - shoes are the original oil cloth; rest of clothes are old, not original

Collection of Mary Worrow

Type: 12" Pair Black Homemade Rag Dolls (circa early 1930s)
Construction: *Body* - floppy soft stuffed polished cotton; jointed at hips; *Features* - embroidered; *Hair* - knotted wool material; *Clothes* - not original

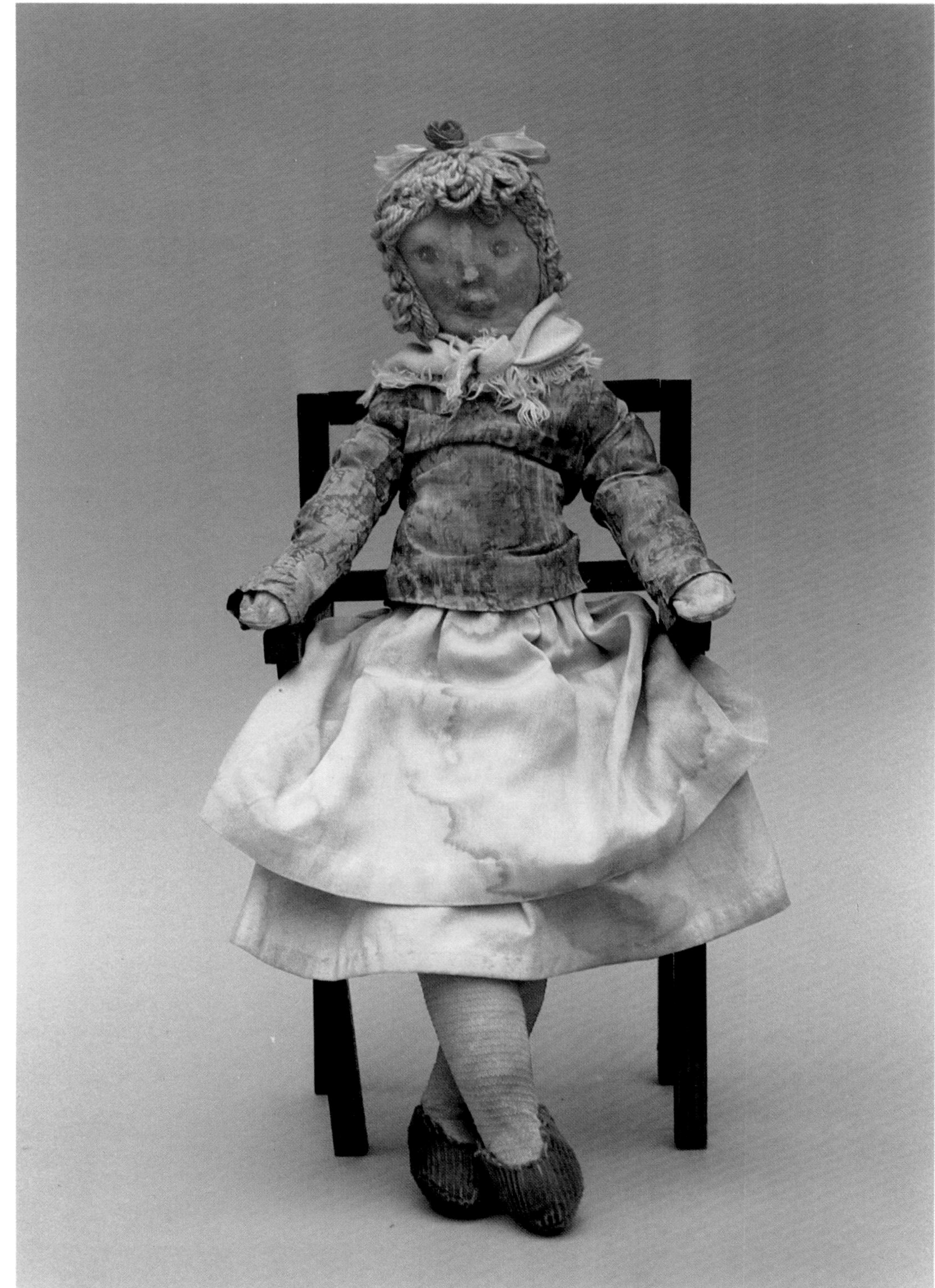

Collection of Margie Kimbro

Type: 17'' Homemade Rag (circa late 1920s, early 1930s)
Construction: *Body* - muslin jointed at hips and shoulders; *Features* - painted (appears to be water color); *Hair* - wool rug yarn sewn onto the head; *Clothes* - all original

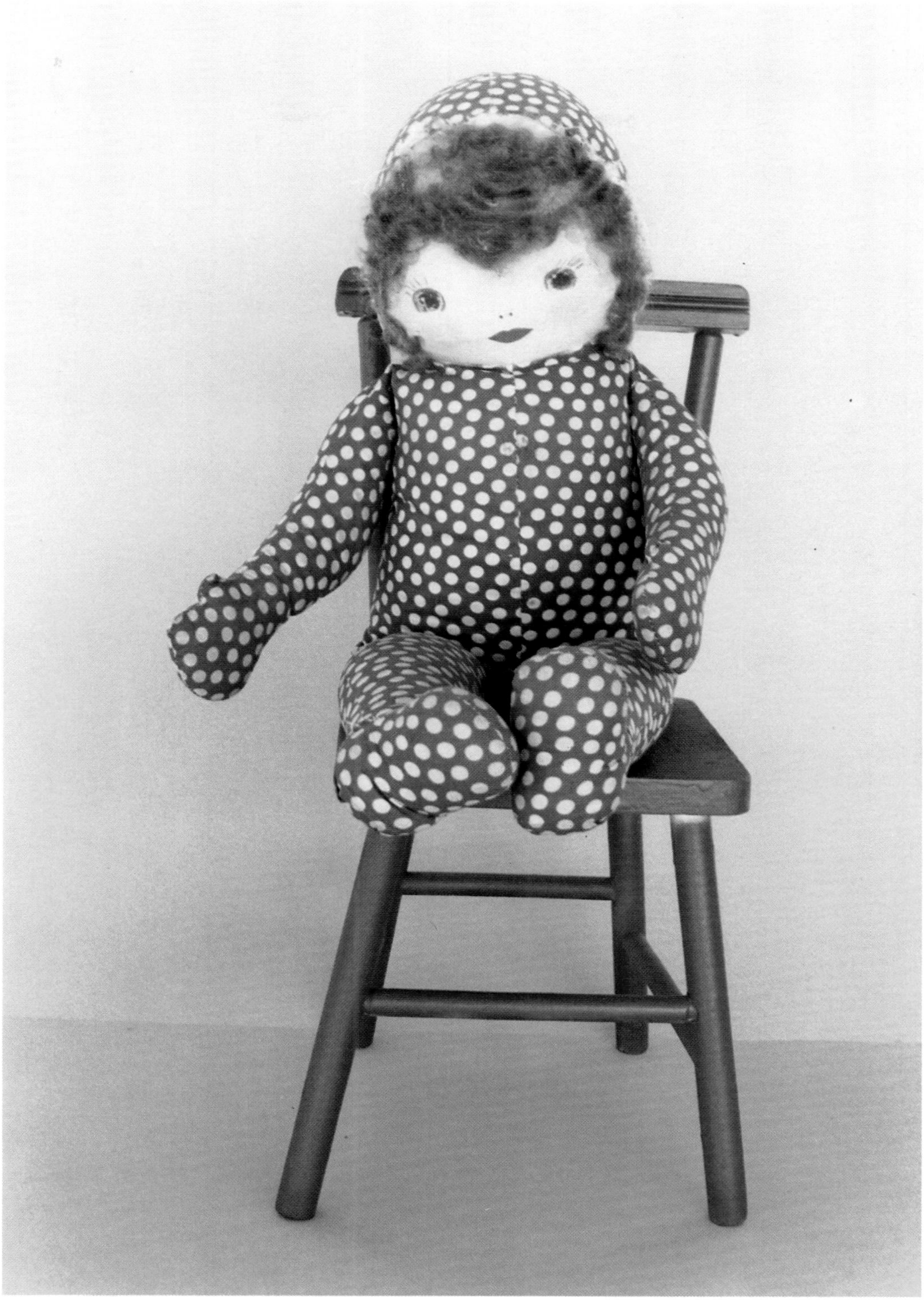

Collection of Charlene Lucinian

Type: 22'' 1940s Manufactured Mask Face Rag
Construction: *Body* - polished cotton stuffed with cotton; *Features* - oil painted onto a mask; *Hair* - mohair applied with glue; *Clothes* - missing

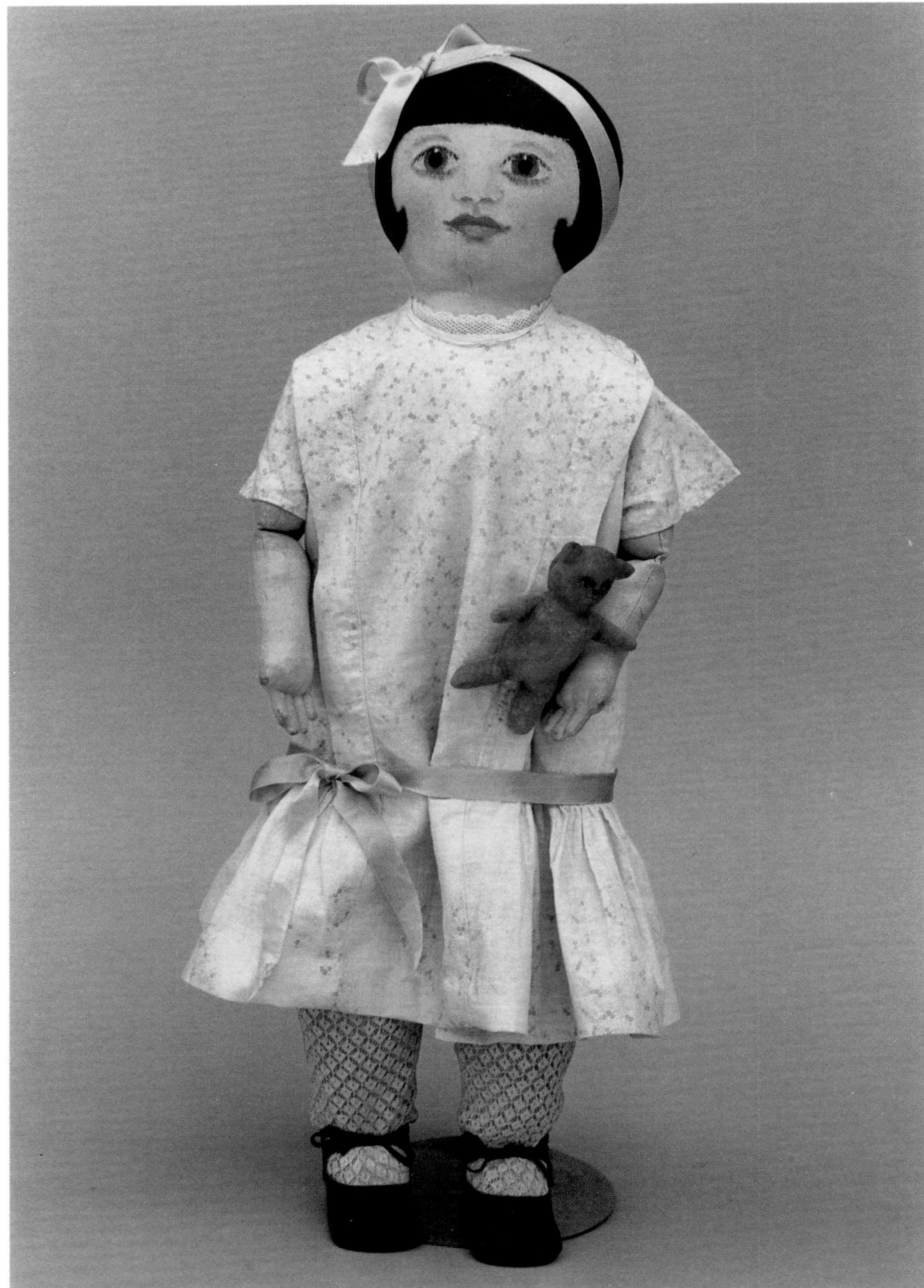

Collection of Mary Worrow

Type: 23" Oil Painted 1920s Rag

Construction: *Body* - muslin stuffed with cotton; jointed shoulders, elbows, knees and hips; fingers and toes stitched; painted extremities; *Features* - oil painted; *Clothes* - original

Clues to Dating: Particular hairstyle that is painted on this doll denotes 1920s era

Collection of Sandra Thompson

Type: 15" Homemade Rag (late 1930s, early 1940s)
Construction: *Body* - this particular type of doll appears to have been made from a pattern; cotton stuffed with cotton; disk jointed extremities; *Features* - embroidered; *Hair* - rug yarn; ears applied; *Clothes* - original

Chapter V

Reproductions

It is common knowledge that whenever a product on the market attains popularity followed by an increase in price, the reproduction will then soon appear. The reproduction makes it easy and affordable to obtain a period rag doll. However, as an investment, it holds no merit. It is important to mention here that one should not confuse a reproduction (copy of an already pre-existing rag doll) with a doll artist original. The originals may very well acquire their own merit in the future, but the purchase is, of course, always speculative.

Reproductions are great to use in decorating a home. They can withstand much more abuse from dust and climate than can an old doll. Most of the reproductions are very well done and signed by the artists. But unfortunately, there are always a few done to deceive. So when in doubt, consider it out!

The following pictures will give a general idea of some of the reproductions and originals on the market at the present time. It is always wise to be familiar with what is new when you're looking for old.

Author's Collection

Type: 15'' Copy of Old Black Doll

Construction: *Body* - new very black sock, polyester thread, stuffed with polyester batting which springs back when squeezed; plastic button eyes; *Clothes* - dressed in old material

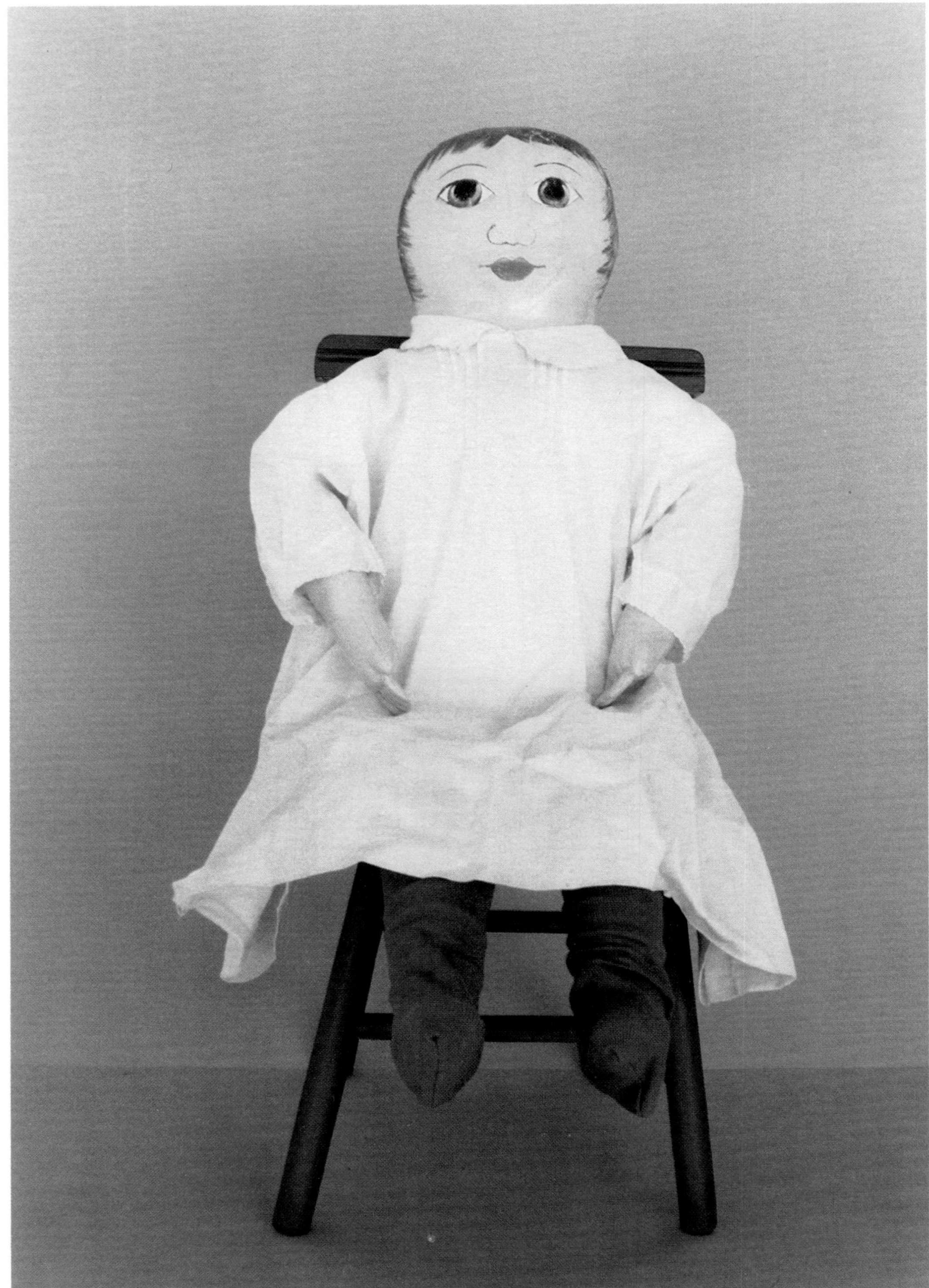

Courtesy of Pippen Hill Antiques

Type: 24" Copy of Old Oil Painted Rag
Construction: *Body* - very white cotton stuffed with polyester batting; very lightweight; no marks; *Features* - facial painting with very shiny latex paint; *Clothes* - old

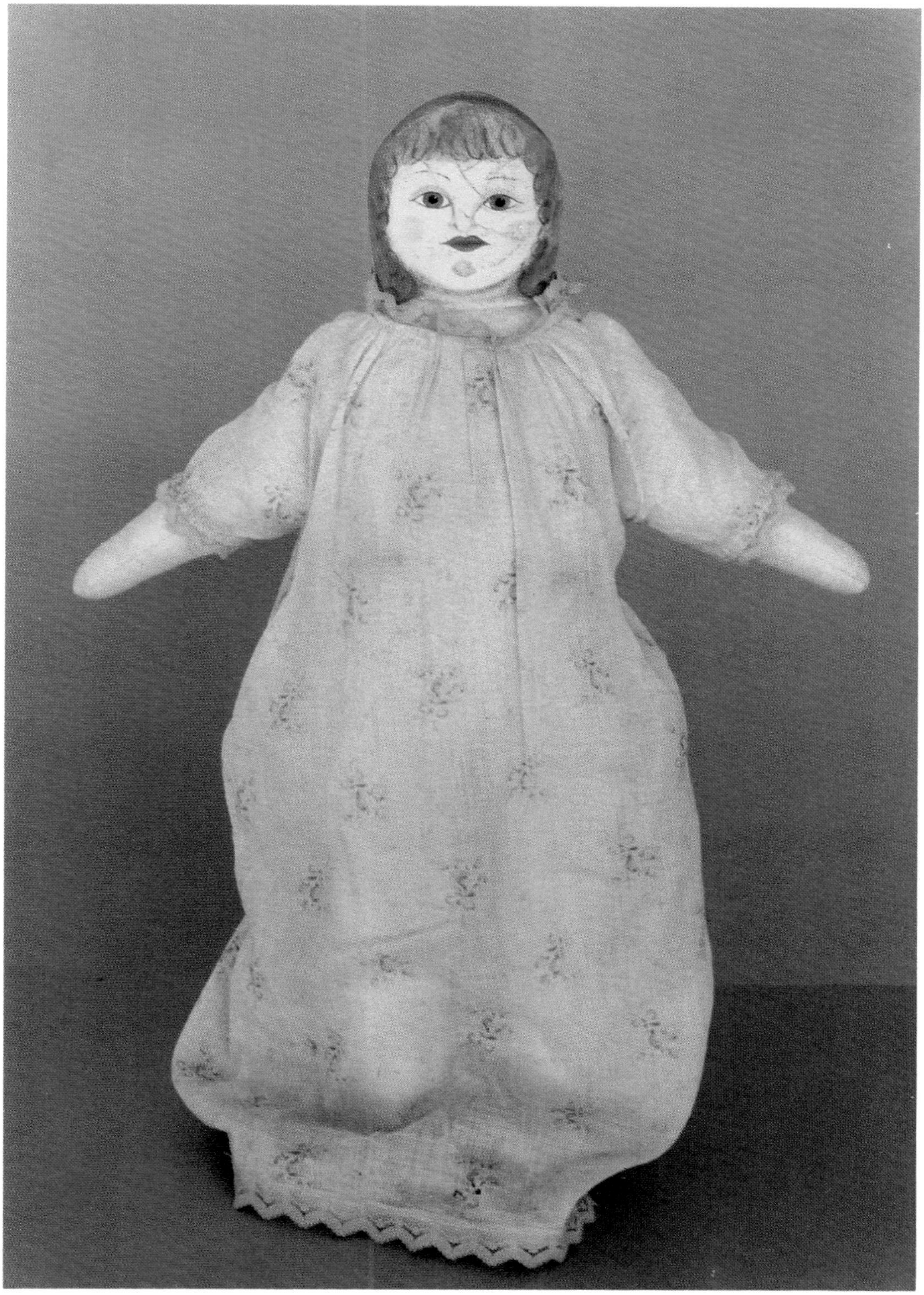

Courtesy of Pippen Hill Antiques

Type: 17½" Copy of Oil Painted Rag
Construction: *Body* - lightweight, very white cotton stuffed with polyester batting; *Features* - done in very inexpensive paint; too white; very obviously new; no marks; *Clothes* - new

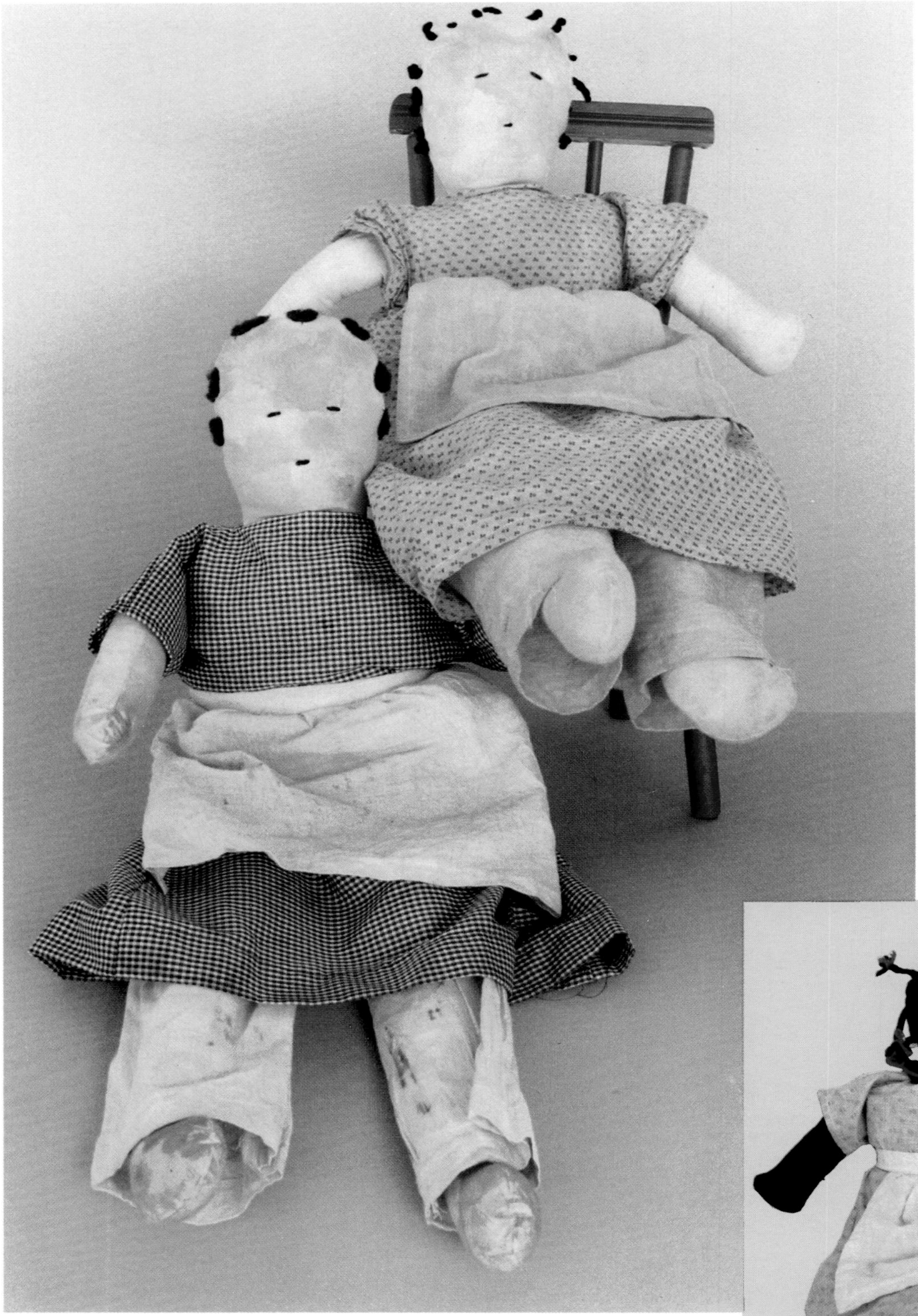

Courtesy of Pippen Hill Antiques

Type: 26'' Betty Hudson Originals; signed on the ''buns''

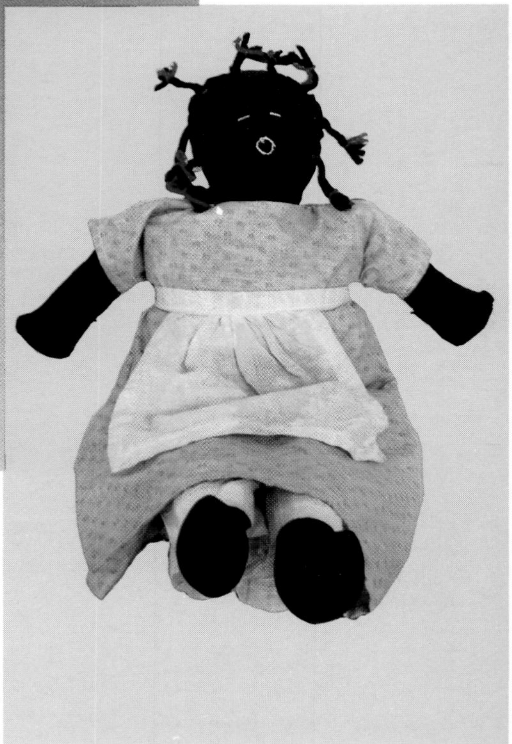

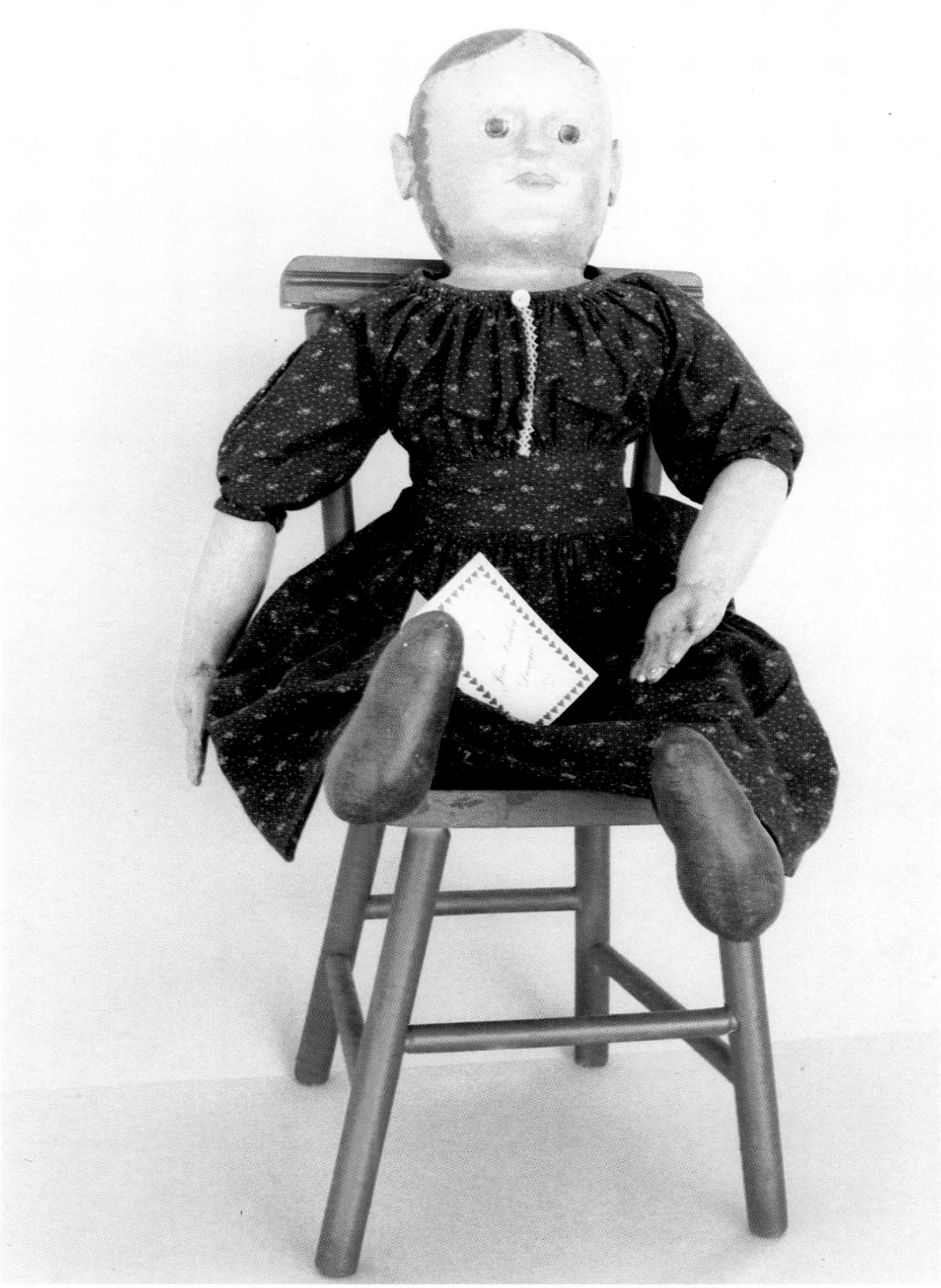

Collection of Charlene Lucinian

Type: 21'' Copy of Izannah Walker by Jan Farley.

Courtesy of Pippen Hill Antiques

Type: 21" Copies of Raggedy Ann & Andy by Folk Dolls & Friends; signed on the "buns".

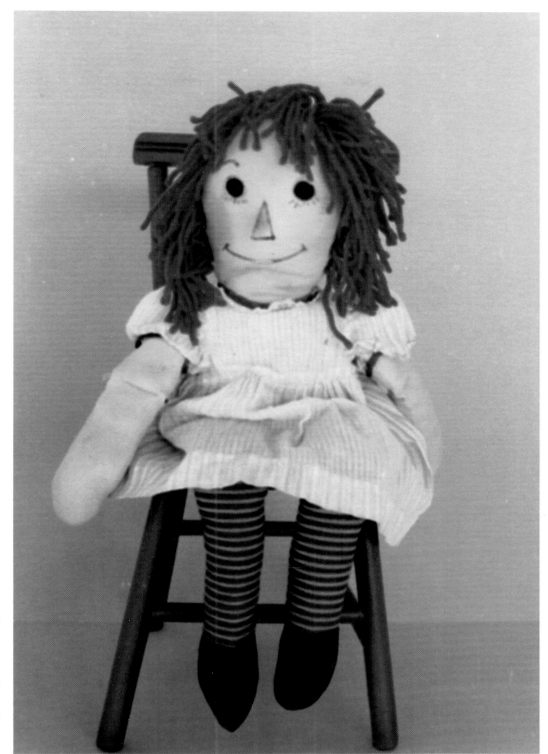

Courtesy of Pippen Hill Antiques

Type: 19'' Floppy Raggedy Ann by Nan
Construction: *Body* - cotton stuffed with batting; jointed at elbows and knees; *Features* - painted, auburn yarn hair

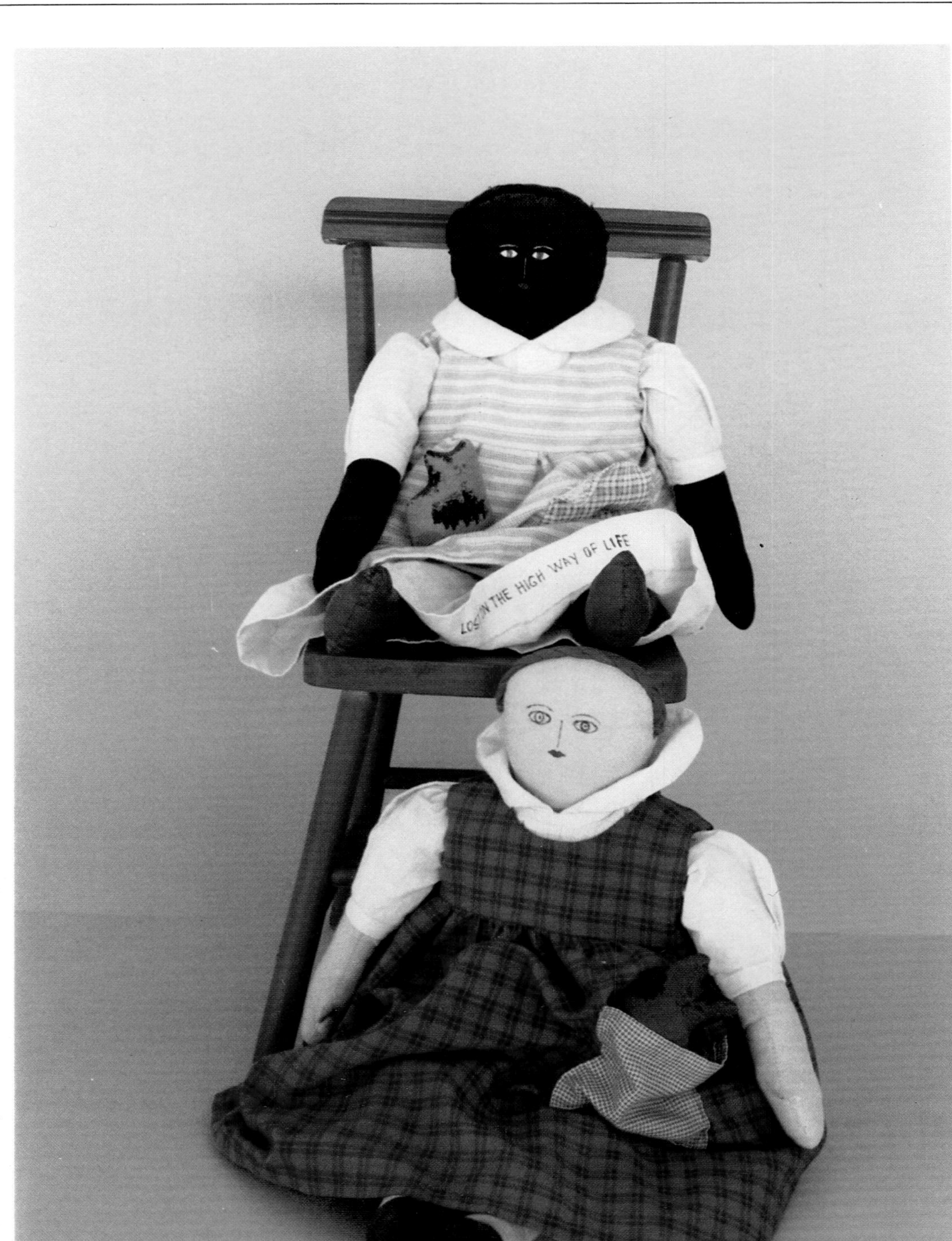

Courtesy of Pippen Hill Antiques

Type: 16" Pair of New Rag Dolls
Construction: *Body* - cotton stuffed with batting; *Features* - stitched

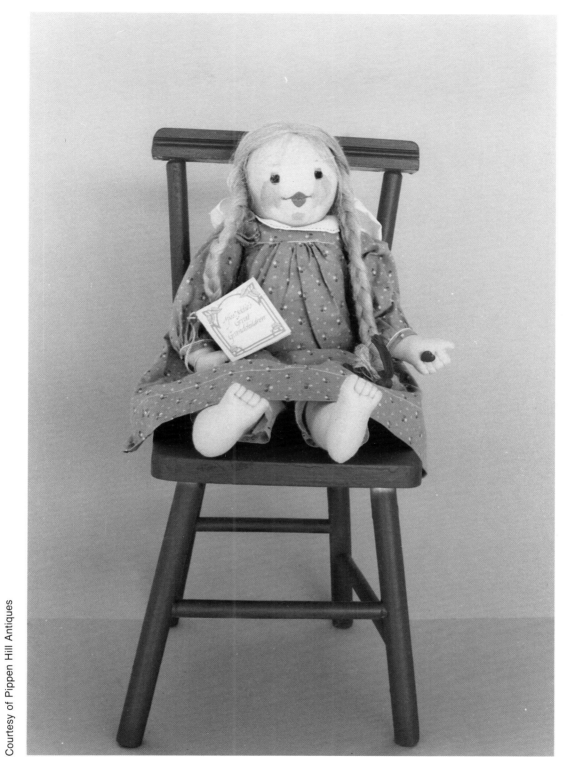

Courtesy of Pippen Hill Antiques

Type: 15" New Painted Face Rag Doll
Construction: *Body* - heavy new cotton; stitched fingers and toes; *Features* - painted; *Hair* - flax

Courtesy of Pippen Hill Antiques

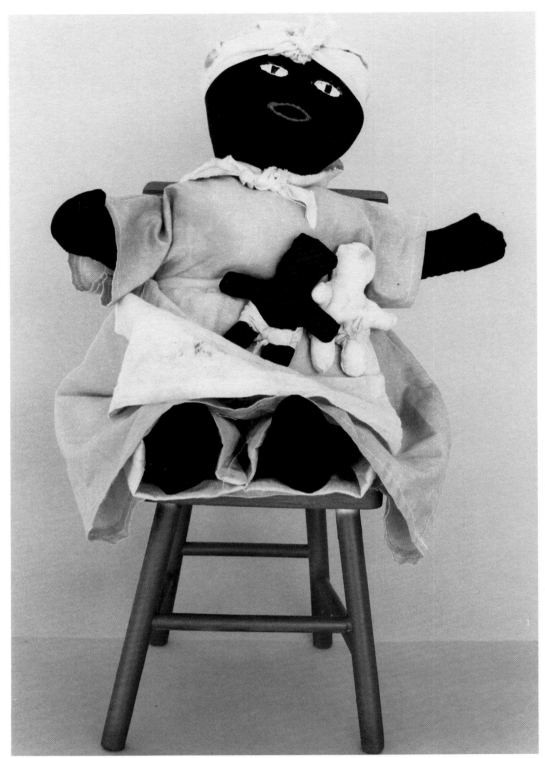

Type: 21" Large Black Mammy (new)

Bibliography

Anderton, Johanna Gast, *Collector's Encyclopedia of Cloth Dolls*

Antique Trader Weekly, *Book of Collectible Dolls*

Coleman, Dorothy S., Elizabeth A., Evelyn J., *Encyclopedia of Dolls Volume II*

Coleman, Dorothy S., Elizabeth A., Evelyn J., *Encyclopedia of Dolls Volume I*

Foulke, Jan, *Blue Book 7th Edition*

Lavitt, Wendy, "American Folk Dolls," *Knopf Collector's Guide to American Antiques Dolls*

Index

American Novelty Manufacturing . . . 89
Alabama Baby . . . 31, 34-38
Art Fabric Mills . . . 31, 39-44
Babyland . . . 31, 47, 48
Beecher . . . 31, 49, 50
Beloved Belindy . . . 75, 85, 87
Black Dolls . . . 18, 38, 50, 56,101, 107, 113, 122
Bruckner . . . 32, 51, 52
Camel with the Wrinkled Knees . . . 75, 88, 90
Chase . . . 32, 53-57
Columbian . . . 32, 58, 59
Fangle, Maude Tausy . . . 32, 60
Farley, Jan . . . 117
Folk Dolls and Friends . . . 118
Gutsell, Ida . . . 32, 61
Heckewelder, Polly . . . 33
Horsman Co. . . . 31, 45
Hudson, Betty . . . 116
Kamkins . . . 32, 62-64
Mask Face . . . 52, 62, 99, 102, 104, 105, 109
Merrie Marie . . . 44
Missionary Rag Baby . . . 31
Mother Congress . . . 33, 65
Moravian . . . 33, 66-68
Multi-face . . . 20
Philadelphia Baby . . . 33, 69
Presbyterian . . . 33, 70, 71
Preservation . . . 8
Primitives . . . 9-29
Raggedy Ann & Andy . . . 75-84, 89, 92-95
  Awake Asleep . . . 82
  Georgene Novelty Co. . . . 80-85
  Gruelle . . . 75-78, 81, 85
  Homemade . . . 92, 94, 95
  Knickerbocker . . . 75, 87, 90, 91
  Mollye's . . . 81
  Volland . . . 75, 76, 79, 86
Raggedy Arthur . . . 91
Reproductions . . . 112-122
Rollinson . . . 33, 72
Sheppard Baby . . . 33
Stuart Baby . . . 33
Sweets . . . 32, 60
Topsy Turvy . . . 48, 52
Uncle Clem . . . 75, 86
Walker, Izannah . . . 21, 33, 73, 74
Washington, George . . . 32, 54

Price Guide

(Prices vary depending on condition of doll)

Page 10
Lifesize Baby $2,500.00-3,000.00

Page 11
30″ Turn of Century Oil Painted Rag . . . $1,500.00-2,000.00

Page 12
36″ Turn of Century Oil Painted Rag . . . $2,000.00-2,500.00

Page 13
24″ Turn of the Century Rag $650.00

Page 14
17″ Late 1800s Oil Painted Rag $650.00-700.00

Page 15
18″ Late 1800s Rag $250.00-350.00

Page 16
17″ Mid 1800s Rag $200.00-250.00

Page 17
22″ Primitive Rag $225.00

Page 18
14″ Early Black Rag $200.00

Page 19
22″ Primitive Homemade Rag $650.00

Page 20
23″ 1870s Multi-Faced Rag $375.00-425.00

Page 21
20″ Oil Painted Rag $1,500.00-3,000.00

Page 22
21″ Early 1900s Rag $250.00-300.00

Page 23
18″ Early Oil Painted Rag $150.00-175.00

Page 24
30″ Mid 1900s Painted Rag $950.00-1,000.00

Page 25
25″ Late 1800s Oil Painted Rag $1,200.00

Page 26
17″ Oil Painted Rag $500.00-650.00

Page 27
22″ Oil Painted Rag $500.00

Page 28
23″ Oil Painted Rag $2,000.00-3,000.00

Page 29
17″ Oil Painted Rag $650.00

Page 34
22″ Alabama Baby $950.00-1,200.00

Page 35
22″ Alabama Baby $1,200.00-1,400.00

Page 36
24″ Alabama Baby $1,200.00

Page 37
14″ Alabama Baby $1,200.00

Page 38
14″ Alabama Baby $1,200.00

Page 39
26″ Art Fabric Girl $175.00-200.00

Page 40
26″ Art Fabric Girl $175.00-200.00

Page 41
16″ Art Fabric $95.00

Page 42
25″ and 8″ Art Fabric Dolls . . . . $325.00 pair

Page 43
18″ Twin Art Fabric Dolls . . . . $250.00 pair

Page 44
30″ Art Fabric Merrie Marie $250.00

Page 45
10″ Lithographed Boy $95.00
12″ Lithographed Girl $125.00

Page 46
26″ Lithograph Girl $225.00

Page 47
30″ Babyland $850.00-1,000.00

Page 48
12″ Babyland $450.00-500.00

Page 49
23″ White Beecher $2,000.00-3,000.00

Page 50
18″ Black Beecher Type $1,800.00-2,000.00

Page 51
14″ Baby Bruckner Doll $450.00

Page 52
12″ Topsy-Turvy Bruckner $350.00-400.00

Page 53
27″ Early Chase Child $950.00-1,000.00

Page 54
25″ George Washington $1,500.00

Page 55
27″ Early Chase $950.00-1,000.00

Page 56
25″ Rare Black Chase $3,500.00-4,000.00

Page 57
16″ Chase Girl $750.00

Page 58
23″ Columbian $2,000.00-2,500.00

Page 59
19″ Columbian $1,500.00-2,000.00

Page 60
24″ Sweets $750.00
14″ Baby $550.00

Page 61
16″ Ida Gutsell Doll $225.00

Page 62
19″ Kamkins $850.00-950.00

Page 63
18″ Kamkins Pair $850.00-950.00

Page 64
18″ Kamkin Baby $1,200.00

Page 65
17″ Mother Congress $150.00

Page 66
16″ Moravian $850.00-1,000.00

Page 67
17″ Moravian Dolls . . . . $1,500.00 pair

Page 68
18″ Moravian Doll $450.00

Page 69
20″ Philadelphia Baby $1,200.00-1,400.00

Page 70
17″ Presbyterian Rag $850.00-1,000.00

Page 71
15″ Presbyterian Rag $75.00

Page 72
17″ Rollinson $475.00

Page 73
20″ Possible Early Izannah Walker $2,500.00-3,000.00

Page 74
15″ Izannah Walker $8,000.00

Page 76
15″ Gruelle Ann $650.00
15″ Volland Ann $500.00

Page 77
15″ Early Raggedy Ann $650.00-800.00

Page 78
15″ Early Raggedy Ann $450.00

Page 79
15″ Volland Andy $500.00

Page 80
18″ Raggedy Ann & Andy $450.00

Page 81
18″ Raggedy Ann & Andy $350.00

Page 82
12″ Awake-Asleep Ann $75.00

Page 83
18″ Raggedy Ann & Andy $175.00-200.00

Page 84
15″ Raggedy Ann $45.00-50.00

Page 85
18″ Beloved Belindy $400.00-450.00

Page 86
17″ Uncle Clem $250.00-300.00

Page 87
15″ Beloved Belindy $150.00

Page 88
Camel with the Wrinkled Knees $50.00

Page 89
15″ Raggedy Copies . . . . $100.00-125.00 pair

Page 90
Camel with the Wrinkled Knees $25.00

Page 91
6″ Raggedy Arthur $15.00

Page 92
19″ Homemade Ann $50.00-75.00

Page 93
18″ Handpainted Raggedies . . . . $350.00 pair

Page 94
18″ Homemade Ann $150.00

Page 95
18″ Homemade Raggedies . . . . $375.00 pair

Page 97
18″ Homemade Rag $35.00-40.00

Page 98
Homemade Rag $65.00

Page 99
24″ Mask Face Rag $65.00-75.00

Page 100
Homemade Boy $65.00

Page 101
Black Rag $45.00

Page 102
22″ Mask Face Rag $75.00-125.00

Page 103
16″ Homemade Rag $75.00-100.00

Page 104
22″ Mask Face Rag $325.00-350.00

Page 105
23″ Mask Face Baby $225.00

Page 106
15″ Rag $75.00-100.00

Page 107
12″ Black Homemade Rags $125.00-150.00

Page 108
17″ Homemade Rag $150.00-175.00

Page 109
22″ Mask Face Rag $25.00-35.00

Page 110
23″ Oil Painted Rag $650.00

Page 111
15″ Homemade Rag $35.00-45.00

Page 113
15″ Black Doll Copy $7.00

Page 114
24″ Oil Painted Rag Copy $15.00-25.00

Page 115
17½″ Oil Painted Rag Copy $10.00-15.00

Page 116
26″ Betty Hudson Originals . . . . No value available

Page 117
21″ Izannah Walker Copy $250.00-350.00

Page 118
21″ Raggedy Ann & Andy Copies . . . . . . No value available

Page 119
19″ Floppy Raggedy Ann . . . . No value available

Page 120
16″ Rag Doll Copies . . . . No value available

Page 121
15″ Painted Face Rag Doll . . . . No value available

Page 122
21″ Mammy . . . . No value available

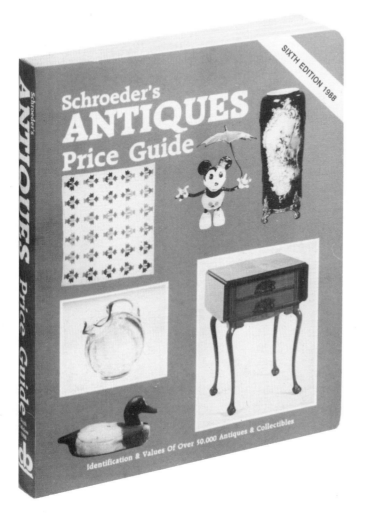